Experiencing the Comfort
of Abba's Love

# I Am His

Rita J. Platt

# NAVPRESS⊘.

NavPress is the publishing ministry of The Navigators, an international Christian organization and leader in personal spiritual development. NavPress is committed to helping people grow spiritually and enjoy lives of meaning and hope through personal and group resources that are biblically rooted, culturally relevant, and highly practical.

**For a free catalog go to www.NavPress.com**
**or call 1.800.366.7788 in the United States or 1.800.839.4769 in Canada.**

ISBN: 978-1-60006-387-9

Cover design by Arvid Wallen
Cover image by Shutterstock

Some of the anecdotal illustrations in this book are true to life and are included with the permission of the persons involved. All other illustrations are composites of real situations, and any resemblance to people living or dead is coincidental.

Unless otherwise identified, all Scripture quotations in this publication are taken from the *Holy Bible, New International Version*® (NIV®). Copyright © 1973, 1978, 1984 by International Bible Society. Used by permission of Zondervan. All rights reserved. Other versions used include: *THE MESSAGE* (MSG). Copyright © 1993, 1994, 1995, 1996, 2000, 2001, 2002. Used by permission of NavPress Publishing Group; and the *Amplified Bible* (AMP), © The Lockman Foundation 1954, 1958, 1962, 1964, 1965, 1987.

Printed in the United States of America

1 2 3 4 5 6 7 8 / 13 12 11 10 09

For Dad

Abba's love is overwhelming.

He healed my heart and then gave you back to me.

Rejoicing in song with you is a gift I'll always treasure.

*Loneliness and the feeling of being unwanted is the most terrible poverty.*

— MOTHER TERESA

Also by Rita J. Platt:

*Step into the Waters*

*An Undivided Heart*

# Contents

# Acknowledgments

I'm overwhelmed when I think about the many women who have granted me the honor of taking part in their journeys. Every one of you has in some way enhanced my ability to see the many shades and textures of Abba's love. Thank you for your courage.

I'm indebted to the voices that nurtured the passion in me to share Abba's love. Thank you, Susan Hamel, for being like a personal cheerleader; I'm braver because of your friendship. Thank you, Terry Behimer, for your words of encouragement. And J. R. and Megan Briggs, you believed in this study and created an opportunity for me to share it with Pierced. Many more, including family members, have extended their support. Thank you so much!

God has placed amazing mentors and pastors in my path. Thank you, Clarice Miller, Gina Carlson, Dot Toeves, Mark Olson, Greg Ralston, and many others, for welcoming me into the church and walking with me as I set out to explore life as a new creation.

There is a core group of women who prayed faithfully throughout this process, keeping me close to their hearts and holding me up. Thank you, Chris Sabin, Susan Hamel, Deb French, Sharon Hagar, Ann Norton, and Debbie Mendoza. I cherish your friendship.

God brought amazing people into my life to walk with and empower me. I am grateful for His gift of Rebekah Guzman, my editor. She connected with the heart of this study and, along with the expertise of the NavPress team, brought it to life. I feel privileged to work with such a talented group of people.

Finally, my husband, Thom, has encouraged me in countless ways. I could not imagine writing without him there to cheer me on. Thanks for the patience and love.

# Abba Father

As we embark on our journey to a place brimming with eternal belonging, I'd like to share a portion of what set me on the path to becoming Abba's precious little girl.

There was a time when I had an earthly daddy who thought I was special, or so it seemed. I remember a time when I misbehaved and my dad and I shared a delightful conspiracy. He was supposed to spank me, but he didn't have the heart to follow through, so he took me over his knee and smacked his hands together loudly. My part was to yell as if I were really being spanked. I grinned like a Cheshire cat, and in my head a little singsong voice said, "Ha-ha, Mom! I'm Daddy's little girl, the apple of his eye."

Then it happened: My world fell apart. I was playing in our apartment when I noticed my dad getting ready to go somewhere. He looked a little uncomfortable, but at the time I thought nothing of it. It seemed like he felt the need to tell me where he was going, and he said, "I'm going to the store to get ice cream." I've always wondered if he ever bought any ice cream that day. I guess it doesn't really matter. What mattered was that he never came home. My daddy was gone! Why, why was he gone?

Later that same evening, my mom discovered a note on her dresser saying that Dad was leaving us. Sobbing and nearly hysterical, she bundled my brothers and me into the car, and we drove around frantically searching for him. Frightened, we all leaned forward and peered out the car windows, straining to see something that would help us find him and make him come home. If we just could have found him, maybe I could have convinced him to come home. I would have behaved better. I would have done just about anything to put things back the way they were. I wanted to yell out, "I love you, Daddy. Please don't leave me!" but I never got my chance to say those words to him. We couldn't find him.

Dazed and feeling helplessly lost and alone, I didn't know what to do or think. As far as I knew, my parents rarely fought. I remembered only one fight. My dad and mom were in the same room but miles away from each other. He sat in a recliner with bloodshot eyes, and my mom sat in a rocking chair crying. I remembered climbing into my mom's lap and being held while she cried. Later I learned that the fight had something to do with my dad being drunk, coming home in the wee hours of the morning, and throwing up all over the front yard. I didn't know then that this scene was a shadow of what was really happening in my dad's life, that he was an alcoholic leading a secret life.

I racked my brain trying to figure out what was happening to us. Questions attacked me, demanding answers. Questions like "Why would he leave us? How could he lie to me like that? What did I do wrong?" I thought, *This can't be real. This is not happening, not to me, not to Daddy's little girl.*

About a week later, my dad came to visit us, but he didn't come alone. We walked outside to meet him and then we saw her: a woman with bright pink lipstick and her son and daughter. Dad introduced us as though it were all completely normal. Did he really expect us to say, "Oh, how wonderful to meet you"? Yet I cooperated and went along, an eleven-year-old already faceless, wearing a protective mask, but inside stung by hurt and betrayal. I wanted to yell at him and I wanted him to hug me all at the same time. I wanted to run at him with fists flailing and hit him right in the stomach, and I wanted to tell him I loved him. I couldn't believe that it was my dad who was doing this. How could he? My hurt sat inside like a rock. *Oh, no! Please, please no! I'm not the apple of my daddy's eye anymore. I've been replaced. He traded me in like some old, useless car. Why would he leave me for them? Why?* That day marked my first plunge into a fatherless abyss of isolation and abandonment.

I saw my dad only a few more times during my childhood and teenage years. He was gone. Birthdays and Christmases came and went without any contact. If I could have put into words all that was in my heart, I would have said, "I'm your daughter. You have to love me. Don't you ever even think about me? Don't you ever wonder how I'm doing, if I get good grades, or what kind of food I like? Don't you want to know me?" The answers to those questions never came, and my heart began to harden. Slowly I began to descend into a murky desolate place. I was filled with painful confusion and a deep-seated sense of being utterly alone.

Years stacked upon years of pain, loss, and poor choices left me empty and aching. Finally, in my late twenties, God dramatically rescued me and made me His own. My heart was captured in a moment as love and peace flooded my being in a way that defies description. I knew in a split second that the gospel was true and was even true for me. The Lord "reached down from on high and took hold of me" (Psalm 18:16). He drew me out of the murky waters and breathed life into me, and I've never been the same.

Not long afterward, God gave me another beautiful surprise: a perfect Father. As a new Christian, I stumbled across this verse: "Though my father and mother forsake me, the LORD will receive me" (Psalm 27:10). A light dawned in the first moment I discovered that God would be my Father and has never dimmed. It's only grown brighter as I settle ever deeper into my place as a daughter of the Most High King.

Whatever your story, whatever happens in your gut when you hear the word *father*, I pray that this study will give you an opportunity to allow God to father you in new ways. As we gaze together on healing images in Scripture of the ultimate Father, may He reveal Himself to you as your perfect Abba Father, full of wisdom, tenderness, and love.

Pause for a moment and jot some notes here or in a journal to describe your personal story, or map out a timeline showing where you are now on your journey. What prompted you to focus some time studying God the Father?

Try meditating on Paul Oakley's song "Father Me." Cry out to God and ask Him for a heart that can receive the kind of fathering described in the following lyrics:

> You have loved me with such perfect love
> Fathered me with such a tender touch
> Your faithfulness surrounds my soul
> Your mercy lifts my head
> How could I repay all you have done?
>
> Father me, faithful Father
> Father me, no one else could ever be
> The perfect Father God to me
>
> You now clothe me with your righteousness
> Hide me in the shadow of your wings
> And even in my darkest days
> Your light will guide my way
> Hallelujah to the King of grace[1]

# Ponder Scripture

There's a popular notion that depicts everyone as God's child. It is true that we are all created by and in the image of God, but what is necessary for us to receive the privilege of being called a child of God? John 1:12-13 says, "To all who received him, to those who believed in his name, he gave the right to become children of God—children born not of natural descent, nor of human decision or a husband's will, but born of God." To become Abba's child, we must receive Jesus—we must choose to believe in Him.

When I first met Marissa, she saw herself as a child of Mother Earth. She explained some of her Wiccan beliefs and then launched into her reasons for rejecting Christianity. Marissa believed that Christianity was all about worshipping a harsh God who arbitrarily throws people into hell and offers no avenue of redemption. No one had ever told her about the God of love, who sacrificially gave His Son so that people could be forgiven. She didn't know she could become a precious child of the One who created all the earth. I explained the wonder of God the Father giving Jesus to pay the penalty for our sin. We talked about His death, His resurrection, and His desire to know her and give her life. The room filled with the fresh scent of hope and new life as Marissa accepted the loving hand extended to her and became a daughter of the King.

If you have already embraced this gift of life, I hope you will simply review the following verses and allow the wonder of the gospel to wash over you in a fresh way. If you have not received the gift of being reborn through belief in Jesus Christ, I hope today will be a new birthday for you. Please read the following verses out loud, personalizing them by putting your name in the blanks:

For God so loved [ _____ ] that he gave his one and only Son, that [if _____ ] believes in him [ _____ ] shall not perish but have eternal life. (John 3:16)

That if [ _____ ] confess[es] with [her] mouth, "Jesus is Lord," and believe[s] in [her] heart that God raised him from the dead, [ _____ ] will be saved. For it is with your heart that you believe and are justified, and it is with your mouth that you confess and are saved. (Romans 10:9-10)

These verses shout out the invitation to a relationship with an amazing God. We accept the invitation by turning to God and admitting our sin and need of forgiveness. We can choose to believe in Jesus, His death on the cross, and His resurrection on our behalf. I consider it an honor to invite you to take your place as a beloved child of almighty God. You can accept that invitation by praying the following prayer:

> *Lord, I know that I have sinned and need the forgiveness and life You offer. I believe that You died to pay for my sins and rose from the dead. I turn away from my old life and turn to You. Please forgive me and grant me courage to walk in the path You have for me. Thank You for making me clean and for blessing me with the privilege of becoming a child of God.*

Whether you celebrated being reborn today or long ago, you were reborn. You were made new. Second Corinthians 5:17 exclaims, "If anyone is in Christ, he is a new creation; the old has gone, the new has come!" You get a "do-over"—you are no longer fatherless, abandoned, or on the outside looking in. Your identity is whole and complete.

Pause for a moment and offer the Lord thanks for the gift of new life. Sing a song, write in your journal, draw a picture, take a walk, or hug a child. Do whatever expresses your heart best.

Our identity as children of God is real, but in the midst of daily life, we accumulate wounds, uncertainty characterizes some relationships, and we forget who we are and where we fit in. Our hearts become clouded with fear, and we resort to wearing masks. Brennan Manning wrote,

 The greatest gift I have ever received from Jesus Christ has been the Abba experience. "No one knows the Son except the Father, just as no one knows the Father except the Son and those to whom the Son chooses to reveal him" (Matthew 11:27). My dignity as Abba's child is my most coherent sense of self. When I seek to fashion a self-image from the adulation of others and the inner voice whispers, "You've arrived; you're a player in the Kingdom enterprise," there is no truth in that self-concept. When I sink into despondency and the inner voice whispers, "You're no good, a fraud, a hypocrite, and a dilettante," there is no truth in any image shaped from that message.[2]

Do Manning's words strike a chord with you? In what way? Would you be more likely to build a self-image by seeking approval or to berate yourself and construct a negative image?

Our true image is revealed in Scripture. Read Romans 8:15-16:

> You did not receive a spirit that makes you a slave again to fear, but you received the Spirit of sonship. And by him we cry, "Abba, Father." The Spirit himself testifies with our spirit that we are God's children.

When we call God *Abba Father*, we are using a term of personal endearment. According to *Strong's Dictionary of Bible Words*, *Abba* is a name "framed by the lips of infants" and "betokens unreasoning trust." When the word *Abba* is paired with Father, "the two together express the love and intelligent confidence of the child."[3] We literally call God "Daddy." Our Daddy is so powerful, yet He tenderly beckons us to cry out to Him with the confidence of a beloved little girl.

Try addressing God as Abba Father. When you speak the words *Abba Father* out loud, what do the words do?

* Have a flat echo
* Stir fear
* Bring about apprehension
* Bring tears to your eyes
* Unveil longings
* Fill you with hope
* Other _____

Read out loud Romans 8:15-16 in Eugene Peterson's translation, *The Message*:

> This resurrection life you received from God is not a timid, grave-tending life. It's adventurously expectant, greeting God with a childlike "What's next, Papa?" God's Spirit touches our spirits and confirms who we really are.

How would you define *timidity*? In what ways might you be timid in your relationship with your Abba Father?

Journal about or draw a picture of what it would look like to live "adventurously expectant, greeting God with a childlike 'What's next, Papa?'" How would your day change? What would greeting each day in this way do to your stress level?

# Reflect

Sometimes it is hard to open ourselves to the Father's touch because we simply don't know what is missing or what fathering could look like. We have no point of reference. Over the next couple of days, be attentive to interactions between fathers and daughters of any age. Are they relating silently, are they interacting boisterously, or do they seem distant? Are they smiling or deep in thought? Watch for fresh glimpses as you skim the latest news or watch a movie. The following are a few observations to get you started:

- A local newspaper published an article about an annual father/daughter dance. Little girls and grown women dressed as

though they were going to the prom were photographed dancing with their daddies.

* The movie *Father of the Bride* shows a doting, protective, and
  often obsessive father reluctantly preparing to give his daughter
  away in marriage.
* The coach in the movie *Remember the Titans* lets his daughter
  encroach on male territory with his welcome and blessing. Her
  daddy refuses to manipulate her, and he includes her in his
  work and his world.
* A young woman watched the easy give-and-take between a
  friend and her dad, noting the display of natural affection.
* Another woman watched a father hurrying through the mall
  and ignoring the attempts of his little girl to catch up or talk to
  him.
* A three-year-old girl buries her head on her daddy's shoulder
  and falls asleep, oblivious to her surroundings.

What observations would you like to add?

Reflect on your collection of images. What tugs at your heart? Where
do you feel raw? What triggers a response you don't understand?

Take note of yearnings that are unearthed and feelings of envy or wistfulness. Which images help you create a template of a loving father/daughter relationship? Pause for a moment to journal your thoughts.

Set aside some time this week to write a description of your "dream dad." Seal it in an envelope and put it aside to be revisited at the end of the study. You may also wish to begin an "Abba scrapbook" and add to it a little each week or use your journal as your scrapbook. I pray that as we continue, you will discover in Scripture images of the perfect Father that will more than fill every empty place in your heart.

# Respond

Psalm 62:8 exhorts, "Pour out your hearts to him, for God is our refuge." Cry out to Him. Bundle up every empty space, hope, dream, moment of pain or elation, and lay them before your Abba Father. If you find it helpful, say them out loud or list them in your journal.

Your Abba Father has heard your cries and is able to use each broken place or happy memory as a window of opportunity to know Him in a new way.

> God can do anything, you know—far more than you could ever imagine or guess or request in your wildest dreams! He does it not by pushing us around but by working within us, his Spirit deeply and gently within us. (Ephesians 3:20, MSG)

Even if you've always seen yourself as fatherless, stuck, orphaned, or unwanted in any way, God is able to embrace you and transform your identity.

Ponder Psalm 18:24:

> GOD rewrote the text of my life
> when I opened the book of my heart to his eyes. (MSG)

Abba can rewrite your story and give you a brand-new life as His cherished daughter. He welcomes you and longs to gather you into His arms. Will you pray with me and open the book of your heart to Him?

> *Abba Father, thank You for rewriting the story of who I am and making me Your very own little girl. Make the truth of who I am as Your child real to me. Take me by the hand and walk me through each moment, giving me eyes to see the many ways You are fathering me. You know my fear and my pain. You know about the aching places no one sees. Please give me courage to open myself more to You each day. Teach me to let down my guard with You, to relate to You with no trace of suspicion. Let Your Word come alive to me and penetrate my heart. I want to live in the delight and freedom of being loved and embraced by You. Amen.*

# Chosen to Belong

Music is one of the few forces in life with the uncanny ability to pierce through my defenses. It lends expression to the real longings of my heart. Years ago, I sat alone and listened over and over to these words of the song "Out Here on My Own":

> Sometimes I wonder where I've been
> Who I am, do I fit in[1]

For a brief time, it was as if my hands were pried away from my ears and echoes of a voice I rarely acknowledged filtered its way through all the noise. As the voice gained momentum, it nicked and eroded the sound barriers that insulated me from any true connection with self or others. Like a blaring siren, the words drew unsolicited attention to my isolation, my drive to prove I was somebody. I experienced emotional release quickly quenched by fear. I dreaded that I was forever destined to be on the outside looking in. Desperation slid through my spirit as I longed to find a way to fit in somewhere, anywhere, to be like the people passing me by who always seemed to have a place where they belonged. I owned a cancerous fear of worthlessness and hungered to feel wanted.

That hunger rumbles in the spirit of others I've been privileged to walk with through painful episodes in their lives. During one climactic moment in her life, I was with Emily and witnessed the shredding of her heart. Emily lived without an active father figure. At age fifteen, she faced a second parental abandonment. Her mother walked into the room where we were talking and perched on the edge of a chair, her whole body tense, ready to spring and attack. With a face lacking any trace of kindness, she glared into Emily's eyes and assaulted Emily with raw hatred, shouting, "I do not want you." Each syllable resounded individually, making the room seem cavernous. The horror of it all unfolded before my eyes as if I were watching a violent torture and murder scene. I still cannot erase Emily's pain from my memory.

The attack was sudden, but the hurtful words were only the beginning. The encounter ended with her mother stalking from the room, every step an emphatic footprint of rejection. That day, Emily's mother followed her father's example and walked out of her life. She crumbled before me, burying her face in her lap as her wounds became audible, filling the room with the sounds of a child in unspeakable pain. She whimpered, "Why would she leave me? Why doesn't she want me?" I had no answers to give, no quick fix to stop the bleeding. I simply stayed, hoping to provide some presence of comfort in the midst of all the leaving.

At one point, Emily and I did talk about God's desire for her to be His child. Her eyes reflected a small flicker of hope crowded by despair and vacancy. She needed time to soak in the possibilities, something to help her absorb a claim of that kind of love. How does someone make a home in the shelter of belonging to Abba when experiences with earthly parents shout, "It can't be true — don't believe it and you won't be disappointed!"

What is your gut reaction to this story? Do you identify with Emily's experience in some way? Were your wounds inflicted blatantly or in a subtle way?

Perhaps you were told without words that you didn't fit in. No matter what your pain, God sees it. There is no hurt too big or too small, too devastating or too insignificant. Wherever you are, God hears and sees every detail of your story. He weeps with you and longs to remove your old identity, the one that screams that you are unimportant, a throwaway, not accepted, unloved, destined to always be alone.

Proclaim aloud the words of Psalm 18:17-19:

He rescued me from my powerful enemy,
 from my foes, who were too strong for me.
They confronted me in the day of my disaster,
 but the LORD was my support.
He brought me out into a spacious place;
 he rescued me because he delighted in me.

What action does your Father take on your behalf?

Your Abba Father is your rescuer. He is able to deliver you from the prison of rejection, from powerful past experiences that hold you down. He wants to bring you to that spacious place where you run free in His love, in His family, because He delights in you. Take that word *delights* into your heart and relish it. Repeat it no matter how unreal it seems. Let it simmer on the back burner as you go through your days, and then uncover it and stir it periodically until it blends so completely that it flows throughout your being.

If you find it nearly impossible to see your heavenly Father as One who delights in you, please hang in there and continue on with this study. Create a little space for God to show His Father heart to you. He is everything you long for. Let Abba bring healing and freedom through the reality of His Word. He wants to enfold you and tuck you into a place in His heart where you will finally find your perfect home. Please pause for a moment and pray with me:

> *God, I'm not sure if I can really call You by the name* Father *without reservation. Please show me who You are. Peel away the fear. Show me where I belong and help me risk believing what seems too good to be true. Rescue me. I want to run free as a daughter who is safe and delighted in. Prepare my heart to receive all You have for me in Scripture. Amen.*

# Ponder Scripture

### Spiritual Adoption

Please take a moment to read the following passages out loud:

> You did not receive a spirit that makes you a slave again to fear, but you received the Spirit of sonship. And by him we cry, "Abba, Father." (Romans 8:15)

Because you are sons, God sent the Spirit of his Son into our hearts, the Spirit who calls out, "Abba, Father." So you are no longer a slave, but a son; and since you are a son, God has made you also an heir. (Galatians 4:6-7)

I will be a Father to you,
and you will be my sons and daughters,
says the Lord Almighty. (2 Corinthians 6:18)

As we saw in the previous week's lesson, because of the gift of Jesus, we are adopted as new babes into the heart of the Father. But what does that really mean? How do we step into our place as daughters of the Lord Almighty? The practice of natural adoption as we know it today does not necessarily provide a full picture of the spiritual adoption seen in Scripture.

In order to bathe in the wonder of belonging to Abba, let's lift the veil of time and peek at some of the characteristics of Roman adoption. In William Barclay's commentary on the book of Romans, he listed the following four results of Roman adoption:[2]

*1. The adopted person lost all rights in his old family and gained all the rights of a legitimate son in his new family. In the most binding legal way, he got a new father.*

Our adoption is complete. Nothing and no one can reverse what God has done. We can honestly claim the Perfect Father as our own Daddy.

*2. It followed that he became heir to his new father's estate. Even if other sons were born afterward, it did not affect his rights. He was coheir with them, and no one could deny him that right.*

Have you ever wondered if God could love you as much as He does your neighbor or Christian friends?

Recently, we brought home a new puppy to the utter dismay of our cat. We definitely have room in our hearts to cherish two pets, but they remain unconvinced. Our home has become a circus as our puppy chases and the cat retaliates with swats and hisses. It is interesting to note that they only behave as archenemies when they think they are competing for space or attention. They both show incredible jealousy even when being petted at the same time. They don't understand that we can love them both even though we are limited by time and space. Our Abba Father is not limited in any way. He has an infinite supply of love. We never need to fear an end to His abundance. His resources are endless. They are not altered or lessened by lavishing His love on all His children. We are all included. Let Ephesians 2:19 reassure you that "you're no longer wandering exiles. This kingdom of faith is now your home country. You're no longer strangers or outsiders. You *belong* here, with as much right to the name Christian as anyone" (MSG).

*3. In law, the old life of the adopted person was completely wiped out; for instance, all debts were canceled. He was regarded as a new person entering into a new life in which the past had no part.*

In the past, you might have identified yourself as an orphan, a defective person, damaged goods or felt so full of shame and regret that you still live under a cloud of exile and darkness. Please hear that as Abba's precious adopted daughter, you have a brand-new identity. You are reborn, you are forgiven, you are clean, you are a child of light, and you are someone who belongs.

*4. In the eyes of the law, he was absolutely the son of his new father.*

Often in our eyes, we miss that we are daughters of our new heavenly Father. If someone could take a picture of how we see ourselves inside, it would be like watching an ad for a "Feed the Hungry" orphan rummaging through the dump. Every painstaking movement we make, the close-up shot of our eyes, conveys a yearning to be lifted out of the filth and taken home yet despairing of ever believing the miracle could happen. But if you have trusted in Christ as your Savior, the miracle has happened. Our adoption is complete. There are no loopholes, no appeals. This is permanent, an eternal adoption.

You are a daughter of God the Father, rescued from the dump, safe in Abba's arms, and no one can snatch you from His hand (see John 10:29).

## Chosen by the Father

In the movie *The Sandlot*, Smalls is the new boy in the neighborhood trying to fit in. Baseball is where the action is with the other boys, but Smalls has very little experience playing baseball. Still, he wants to be included with the other kids, so he shows up with his glove, gulps, and plunges in like a fish trying to swim upstream. The kids do what they've done for years: They size up one another and choose who they want on their team, the first pick happening quickly, decisively, and jubilantly. Then, as the pickings get slim, the pace slows down and Smalls is left standing there. Reluctantly, a team agrees to take him; he is chosen dead last.

Have you ever lived out that scene or watched one like it unfold? Some kids have confidence spilling all over their faces, some try on a look of indifference, while others seem fascinated by the ground, eyes downward and feet kicking the dirt. It is one of the most agonizing moments on the playground or in gym class. Was there ever a time when you didn't get chosen for something or a time when you were chosen last? How did you feel? How did you allow your inward feelings to be expressed?

Sometimes we approach Abba with the dread of being the last one chosen or the only one left out. Yet when our Abba Father adopts us, we are not standing in some group waiting, holding our breath, hoping against all hope that someone will want us. Linger over Ephesians 1:3-6 for a few minutes:

> Praise be to the God and Father of our Lord Jesus Christ, who has blessed us in the heavenly realms with every spiritual blessing in Christ. For he chose us in him before the creation of the world to be holy and blameless in his sight. In love he predestined us to be adopted as his sons through Jesus Christ, in accordance with his pleasure and will—to the praise of his glorious grace, which he has freely given us in the One he loves.

I'm filled with wonder at the thought of being chosen in accordance with His pleasure. God didn't reluctantly adopt us; He chose us on purpose. There's no sense here of "Oh, do I have to take *her*?" On the contrary, the original word used for pleasure, *eudokia*, implies "delight, kindness, wish" or a "gracious purpose."[3]

Now revisit verses 4 and 5 in the *Amplified Bible*. Let the words roll slowly from your lips. Deliberately speak each word out loud:

> Even as [in His love] He chose us [actually picked us out for Himself as His own] in Christ before the foundation of the world, that we should be holy (consecrated and set apart for Him) and blameless in His sight, even above reproach, before Him in love.
>
> For He foreordained us (destined us, planned in love for us) to be adopted (revealed) as His own children through Jesus Christ, in accordance with the purpose of His will [because it pleased Him and was His kind intent].

Pause and journal your thoughts and feelings as you meditate on the truth that God chose you on purpose to be His child.

Today, selecting and adopting a child often require tremendous planning and sacrifice, yet no one can match the price your heavenly Father paid to make you His own. 1 Peter 1:18-20 says,

> You know that it was not with perishable things such as silver or gold that you were redeemed from the empty way of life handed down to you from your forefathers, but with the precious blood of Christ, a lamb without blemish or defect.

Your Abba Father intentionally gave His own Son. God tied His own hands as He looked on His Son's suffering. He put Himself through that agony so that you and I could become His daughters.

Sit quietly for a few moments. Enter the silence and open your heart to the truth that you are a wanted child. Take it in until it begins to ooze out of your pores. Say to yourself over and over, "I am a wanted child."

## Reflect

As you read the following passages, underline any words or phrases that highlight Abba's tender claim on your heart.

> You also were included in Christ when you heard the word of truth, the gospel of your salvation. Having believed, you were marked in him with a seal, the promised Holy Spirit, who is a deposit guaranteeing our inheritance until the redemption of those who are God's possession—to the praise of his glory. (Ephesians 1:13-14)

> I have engraved you on the palms of my hands;
>    your walls are ever before me. (Isaiah 49:16)

## A Commemorative Birthmark

You and I are marked as God's children. We are somebody; we matter. We have a place of honor, a loving eternal home. Never again do we need to live like one who is excluded or ignored. Still, day to day, in the midst of brokenness, it's hard to keep the truth in front of us. We need help remembering that we belong.

Consider finding or creating a birthmark and taking it out often to remind yourself that you belong to the Father. For example, purchase a simple ring and have it engraved with the inscription "Daddy's little girl" or create a birth certificate naming God as your Father. Kylie shared her wish that her daddy would buy her a pretty dress. She decided to buy a beautiful dress. She searched for and found the perfect dress. Whenever she sees it hanging in her closet or wears it, she is reminded that she is a chosen and precious child of God.

My marker is a sculpture of a father and daughter. The daughter is curled up and nestled next to her daddy. Her head is turned to gaze up at him as she leans into his arm. I imagine myself formed into that position with my heavenly Daddy. I snuggle close and look to Him for life, wisdom, and love. It's a safe and hopeful reminder of where I belong. I have a place, an eternal home, in my Abba's arms.

# Respond

## A New Name

As a child of a King fitting securely into the niche of my Abba's eternal embrace, I have a new song to sing. I'm no longer sitting alone crying out songs laced with desperation; now I'm one of the chosen ones, celebrating my adoption into my Father's heart. A new melody resonates deep in my spirit. The words of a song by D. J. Butler, "I Will Change

Your Name," expresses a new hope alive and flourishing in me:

> I will change your name,
> You shall no longer be called
> wounded, outcast, lonely or afraid.
> I will change your name,
> Your new name shall be
> confidence, joyfulness, overcoming one,
> faithfulness, friend of God, one who seeks My face.[4]

What are some new names your Abba Father might have for you? Picture yourself becoming a person who reflects your new name. What might that look like in your daily life?

Please pray with me:

*Father, words don't express what I feel. I don't really know how to say thank You. I don't know if I really comprehend the magnitude of the price You paid to make me Your own. I want to embrace this new place, this new home You've given me. I need You, Abba. Help me when old fears terrorize me; remind me that I'm Your precious child. Please hold me and take me deeper and deeper into the wonder of being wanted. I love You. I praise You. I choose to take You at Your word. Teach me to live as a chosen daughter of the Most High King. Amen.*

# The Father's Love

God loves you. Has anyone ever aimed those words directly at you? I was twenty-nine years old when I first heard those words. At the time, all I could do was blurt out, "Yeah, right." I told myself it was only an empty cliché, but I couldn't resist an almost magnetic pull to investigate further. Could it really be? Did a God exist who loved me? Not long afterward, through a dramatic sequence of events awash in grace, I met the Lord for the first time. It was as if the universe stood still as a love that defies description flooded every inch of my being.

I've never been able to put adequate words to that moment, but sometimes a song comes close. There is an old hymn titled "The Love of God" that brings my heart and imagination together with its beauty. Pause for just a moment and read the lyrics or sing them if you know the melody. Let your imagination run free and allow it to make the rich images in the song visible as you contemplate the vastness of God's love.

> The love of God is greater far than tongue or pen can ever tell
> It goes beyond the highest star and reaches to the lowest hell
> The guilty pair, bowed down with care, God gave His Son to win
> His erring child He reconciled and pardoned from his sin

Could we with ink the ocean fill and were the skies of parchment made
Were every stalk on earth a quill and every man a scribe by trade
To write the love of God above would drain the ocean dry
Nor could the scroll contain the whole, though stretched
from sky to sky

O love of God how rich and pure, how measureless and strong
It shall forevermore endure the saints' and angels' song.[1]

Does this song resonate in your heart? Or are you saying, "Yeah, right"? Maybe you are caught somewhere between; maybe you want to believe the words, but right now wistfulness is all you manage to feel. No matter which way you're leaning, this week I invite you take a risk and a closer look at God's love. Try to crack open a window in your heart and explore love with me.

## Ponder Scripture

We often toss the word *love* around so freely. We love chocolate, hearts, flowers, chick flicks, sleeping in, and watching *CSI*. The list is endless. Have you ever picked daisy petals while reciting, "He loves me, he loves me not," and then repeated the whole process until you got the answer you wanted? Is love that random or easily manipulated? Is it complex, simple, or both? What about the phrase "Love means never having to say you're sorry"? Is that true? Is love something that is given and then withdrawn when we are replaced? All of these questions and sayings expose our ongoing struggle to wedge something as big as love into a definition.

Still, we will accept the challenge and attempt to describe not only love but also Abba's love, keeping the edges of our definition elastic and breathable. We can make a beginning by piecing together God's word pictures of love in Scripture. Read 1 Corinthians 13:4-8 and start a preliminary sketch of what loving actions look like by listing some ideas in the chart below.

| What Love Does | What Love Does Not Do |
|---|---|
|  |  |
|  |  |
|  |  |
|  |  |
|  |  |
|  |  |
|  |  |
|  |  |
|  |  |
|  |  |
|  |  |

Read the same passage in *The Message*:

Love never gives up.
Love cares more for others than for self.
Love doesn't want what it doesn't have.
Love doesn't strut,
Doesn't have a swelled head,
Doesn't force itself on others,
Isn't always "me first,"
Doesn't fly off the handle,

Doesn't keep score of the sins of others,
Doesn't revel when others grovel,
Takes pleasure in the flowering of truth,
Puts up with anything,
Trusts God always,
Always looks for the best,
Never looks back,
But keeps going to the end.

Love never dies.

Now add any additional nuances, shades, or colors of love to your sketch.

Looking back through the passage, we find a key element of Abba's love in verse 8, "Love never fails." In the Psalms alone I count twenty-six times where God's love is referred to as unfailing. It isn't frivolous or fleeting. It cannot disappear, fade away, weaken, fall short, or become absent. As God's daughters, we are loved forever and cannot be separated from His love. Romans 8:37-39 says,

> None of this fazes us because Jesus loves us. I'm absolutely convinced that nothing—nothing living or dead, angelic or demonic, today or tomorrow, high or low, thinkable or unthinkable—absolutely nothing can get between us and God's love because of the way that Jesus our Master has embraced us. (MSG)

The unending sacrificial nature of His love could frame our picture, be the background image, the very paper we draw on, the ink we use, and still not say it strongly enough. Nothing can separate us from His love.

That kind of love, God's unfailing love, is radically different from what many of us have experienced. Hannah shared with me her struggle to associate verses like these with the Father's love. She could swallow the idea that Jesus loves her and died for her, but she survived such abuse at the hands of her earthly father that the concept of God as Father became scary and unthinkable. Painful images, still raw and seeping, were all she had to attach to the word *father*.

Hannah felt there was too much risk involved in placing any hope in a father figure. What if she went away disappointed again? Could her heart survive the process of getting to know Abba? It took some time and incredible courage for her to sift through and separate her past experience from who God is, to not make God in the image of her earthly father. She needed to purposefully suspend any preconceptions and let hope be planted in her heart. Then she began the task of building a whole new repertoire of images to correspond to encountering God as a perfect Father.

Can you relate to Hannah's dilemma? If so, in what ways? Would you be willing to wipe the slate clean and start afresh to allow new healing images of Abba Father to be formed? If you are not at the point of willingness yet, would you pause and ask the Lord to give you an open heart?

If, like Hannah, you feel somewhat receptive to the possibility that Jesus loves you, begin your new collection of pictures by meditating on the following verses. In John 14:9, Jesus said, "Anyone who has seen me has seen the Father." Colossians 1:15 calls Jesus the "image of the invisible God," and Hebrews 1:3 says that "the Son is the radiance of God's glory and the exact representation of his being."

As you experiment with absorbing the vision of a loving heavenly Father, keep in mind that both the strong and tender impressions you have of Jesus reflect your Father's heart.

Mull over John 10:9-15 and 27-30. What attributes do you see in Jesus in these verses?

Have you ever blended your idea of a loving Shepherd with the heart of the Father? Take some time to journal your thoughts, fears, questions, and feelings, and then commit them to the Lord.

Ask your Father to give you eyes to see Him and to bring His image a little more into focus each day.

As we use Scripture to piece together a basic composite of Abba's love, we begin unveiling its beauty and integrity. Why, then, do we still often find ourselves feeling empty and unloved? Why can't we just accept His love and ignore the past? What makes it so difficult to receive His love and allow it to transform our lives? Over the years, I've listened as a number of young women have bared their souls and, in doing so, have shed light on these questions. Listening to their input illumines for me the need to continue perfecting our pictures by adding detail and color to our rough draft.

Tiffany shared with me a major roadblock for her. She said, "I know all the concepts, John 3:16 and other verses, in my head, but there's some kind of disconnect. It's not part of my heart. God gave Jesus for everyone and I'm just one of millions He died for. I don't see how that makes me special or cherished in the way you talk about." It was as if she was begging me, "Please tell me someone loves me personally. Tell me I matter to somebody in a way that's unique and different from what I've lived so far."

In what ways do you view yourself as personally loved by God the Father or as one of the many?

To Tiffany and any of you who feel unseen or lost in the crowd, I cannot say it emphatically enough: The Father's love for you is *personal*. He knows the number of hairs on your head (see Matthew 10:30). He wants to make His home in you and include you in the intimacy and oneness shared between Himself and Jesus (see John 14:23). The Father holds you securely in His hand, and no one can snatch you from that place of intimacy (see John 10:28). He created you in all your uniqueness and cherishes you as His precious daughter. Your name is engraved on His heart. His love for you is far from a generic prescription handed out thoughtlessly to the world. Ask Him to make you aware of the intimate nature of His love for you. Watch and listen for His love and record any fresh realizations of His care in your journal.

Some of us struggle to receive God's love because it's like nothing we've ever known or have any point of reference for knowing. We don't have any foundational experience in our repertoire to help us comprehend a love so great. It's as though we're stranded in a foreign country and don't speak the language.

In the movie *Mr. Holland's Opus*, Mr. Holland is a man whose life is infused with music. He is a composer working on his masterpiece and a music teacher imparting his passion for music to hundreds of students, yet his son, Cole, is deaf and there's a tremendous language barrier between them that Mr. Holland feels helpless to overcome. A scene in the movie that comes when Cole is older shows Cole and Mr. Holland entrenched in a conflict that exposes the frustrating nature of their relationship. Their battle gives birth to a new avenue of communication. Cole shows his dad a way he can enter into the language of music. He cranks up the volume and sits with his legs draped over the speakers, feeling the sound. Mr. Holland and his son learn to connect in a powerful new way.

Maybe when you hear someone say, "God loves you," you don't get past the echo of the words. Maybe you need to hear it in a new way or learn the language of love. If you feel as if you are deaf to the Father's love, experiment with creative new ways of hearing and receiving. Expose yourself again and again to the foreign sounds until you can make out a word here or there. Don't be concerned if nothing seems familiar at first or if you don't understand every word. Choose one of the following exercises as a means of immersing yourself in a new culture, a place inhabited by the love of your Father:

- Begin a love journal. You can use a simple notebook or whatever form of journal you want; just keep it available and record what touches your heart. One possible example would be to watch the movie *The Notebook* and observe the relationship between Noah and Allie. Later in life, Allie gets Alzheimer's. When she can no longer remember their lives together, Noah reads her their love story. Sometimes she has brief flashes of remembrance. Noah relishes those moments, but she pulls away and forgets him again. Still, he never gives up. What is it about Noah's love for Allie that brings out the Kleenex? Is it his perseverance, the unfailing nature of his love for her regardless of her ability to reciprocate, or something else? Briefly record your thoughts.

- As you go through your days, make note of anything that surprises you with a tear. Whenever a moment, experience, song, movie, or interaction moves you, record it in your journal as an artifact of the language and culture of love. Let it sink in as you create a dictionary of this new language.

♦ Draw yourself a word picture of God's love.

Read Psalm 103:8-13 and then reread verse 11. Step outside, gaze up at the sky, and meditate on the truth that "as high as the heavens are above the earth, so great is his love for those who fear him." Ask yourself, *How high are the heavens? Is the distance even measurable?* Be still and repeat the verse out loud as you gaze at the heavens. Try doing the same exercise at night. Does that affect you any differently?

Sometimes it's difficult to receive love because our loss takes up too much space. Mull over the words of Psalm 103:13. How do you feel about the comparison of an earthly father to the heavenly Father?

Do you sense the need to grieve the loss of a compassionate earthly father in order to open your heart to receive your heavenly Father's love? If so, allow yourself to mourn.

Acknowledge the times you longed for your father to express his love. Take out each painful memory and express it in your journal through words or drawings. Write a letter to your father that is for your eyes only. On paper, ask the questions that plague you. Ask the "Why" questions. A wise counselor once suggested I do this very thing, and I agreed, thinking, *No big deal. I'm a good Christian and, of course, I've forgiven my dad.* When I actually put pen to paper, I came away shocked at the depth of anger and hurt I still carried inside me. Somehow spilling my brokenness, essentially bleeding all over that piece of paper, was a cathartic step in my healing process. I admitted my hurt and then began to bring it before my Abba Father.

Psalm 62:8 says, "Pour out your hearts" to God, so bring all your pain and expose it, lay it out before Abba. Sit quietly with open hands and ask your Abba Father to help you receive all He has for you as you work through this Bible study. Tell Him you need His healing, you need Him to make Himself real to you. Ask Him to apply the soothing balm of His love and breathe into your heart the truth and life of His Word. Take some time to be still before moving on.

Women I've met with have shared some of the ways they struggle to feel and receive Abba's love. Other women recount yet another obstacle to receiving love: carrying around a continuous sensation that there must be something inherently wrong with them. They feel abandoned and ignored, physically or emotionally, by their earthly fathers and hold a sense of rejection so deeply inside that it becomes part of their identity. They live with the belief that they are fatally flawed or so defective that they're unworthy of love.

Laurie sees herself stuck on an unending treadmill of performance and perfectionism. She wears herself out trying to rise to some impossible standard in order to prove herself worthy. Kelly simply stops trying to perform and becomes engulfed in a sense of worthlessness. Some of us get caught in an alternating cycle of perfectionism and giving up that leaves us feeling like a continual failure. Often as we become children of God, we translate all this into a performance-based Christianity that cannot allow us to embrace the luxury of unconditional love.

With our perfect Father, the good news is that He doesn't expect us to earn His love. We aren't loved by Him because of our performance or because we've earned some elusive spiritual status. He knows it all, good and bad, and He still chooses to save us and bring us into His family as beloved daughters.

Read Titus 3:4-7 and Ephesians 2:4-5. What do these verses say about why God saves us?

Next, meditate on these words from Romans 5:8: "God demonstrates his own love for us in this: While we were still sinners, Christ died for us." The Father's love doesn't consist of empty words or nice-sounding phrases. He *demonstrates* His love. He puts action behind His words. Shakespeare once said, "They do not love that do not show their love."[2] Your Father shows His passionate pursuit of your heart by sacrificing His only Son for you. He took the first step toward giving you a new foundation to live life from, and you are not required to climb the steps to Him. His love is unconditional, a love that transforms you and grants you self-respect in the place of shame. That's a love beyond our wildest dreams that cannot be earned or lost.

Consider this quote from Oswald Chambers that describes God's love:

> The bedrock of our Christian faith is the unmerited, fathomless marvel of the love of God exhibited on the Cross of Calvary, a love we never can and never shall merit. . . . Undaunted radiance is not built on anything passing, but on the love of God that nothing can alter. The experiences of life, terrible or monotonous, are impotent to touch the love of God, which is in Christ Jesus our Lord.[3]

Journal about any ways in which you've been starved for that kind of Fatherly love and affection. Perhaps you could identify some possible sources of your hunger, events that brought about your feelings, or times you needed to experience unconditional love.

Anna Dula was held prisoner at Auschwitz during World War II. Her captors nearly starved her there, and in her desperation she tried to steal a potato. She was caught and punished severely. She was denied food for more than a week. Again and again, Anna faced inhuman deprivation. At times, she survived by eating only dead grass and tree bark.

When the Allies finally liberated Anna and her fellow prisoners, they lavished rich food on everyone, even chocolate. As a result, many became ill because it had been so long since their stomachs were exposed to real food.[4]

Maybe, like Anna, you want to fill up with the richness, the "chocolate," of God's love immediately but can't quite digest it yet. You may need to take in small amounts at first. Begin with pure spiritual milk and taste and see that the Lord is good (see 1 Peter 2:2). If you are at a place of diving in and experiencing every taste and texture, by all means relish every bite. But if you are not there yet, begin with a steady diet, one sip or spoonful at a time, of true love that ultimately leads you to a feast of wonder and freedom.

Read the following verses and choose one that matches most with where you are right now on your journey with God:

- Psalm 23:6
- Psalm 33:5
- Psalm 63:3-5
- Psalm 86:5,15
- Psalm 136:1-26
- Jeremiah 31:3
- 1 John 3:1
- 1 John 4:16-18

Each day for the next week, simply read the verse you chose aloud. Ask God to write it on your heart as you sit in silence for a few minutes. Don't worry if there's no momentous revelation or if you don't feel something—simply take in a steady diet of truth. Your spirit is being nourished even if you don't see immediate evidence.

# Reflect

Psalm 33:6 says, "By the word of the LORD were the heavens made." Contemplate for a moment the creative power of words. What positive words were spoken to you in the last week? Are negative words more plentiful and easier to remember?

Angela confided that not only had she never heard the words "I love you" spoken by her father, he'd actually voiced the opposite. He'd told her how he hated her and wanted nothing to do with her ever again. As she spoke, her eyes gave away how haunted she was by those words. She longed for something that never existed for her, a father's tender words.

The old saying "Sticks and stones will break my bones, but words will never hurt me" is a farce. Words carve out festering wounds, and so does the lack of words.

Another woman shared her hunger for her daddy to say those three life-giving words, "I love you." She said, "I think he may have loved me in some way, but I so longed to hear him say it."

What about you? Do you long to hear words of love spoken to you? What might be created in you if you could hear God speak the following words from Isaiah 54:10 to you?

"Though the mountains be shaken
    and the hills be removed,
yet my unfailing love for [your name] will not be shaken
    nor my covenant of peace be removed,"
    says the LORD, who has compassion on [your name].

Your heavenly Father extends His love to you in many ways. You are treasured by Him. He even sings over you with delight. Reflect on the words of Zephaniah 3:17:

> The LORD your God is with you,
>     he is mighty to save.
> He will take great delight in you,
>     he will quiet you with his love,
>         he will rejoice over you with singing.

Proclaim them out loud. Experiment with paraphrasing and personalizing this verse in your journal. Then allow yourself to imagine climbing into Abba's lap. Picture Him tenderly stroking your hair, quieting you with His love, and singing over you. What noise in you needs to be quieted? What song would you like Him to sing? Take some time to bask in the warmth of His love.

# Respond

Ponder the following quote from Catherine of Genoa's life and teachings.

> I have seen this love. Indeed, every day I feel myself more occupied with him and I feel a greater fire within. It is as if I have given the keys of my house to Love with permission to do all that is necessary.[5]

Can you ever see yourself giving the keys of your house to Love?
Read Psalm 13:5-6 and ask your Abba Father to make each word true in your daily experience.

I trust in your unfailing love;
>   my heart rejoices in your salvation.

I will sing to the LORD,
>   for he has been good to me.

Sing your favorite worship or love song to your heavenly Father.

# A Special Note

My heart's cry for you is recorded in Ephesians 3:14-21:

> I kneel before the Father, from whom his whole family in heaven and on earth derives its name. I pray that out of his glorious riches he may strengthen you with power through his Spirit in your inner being, so that Christ may dwell in your hearts through faith. And I pray that you, being rooted and established in love, may have power, together with all the saints, to grasp how wide and long and high and deep is the love of Christ, and to know this love that surpasses knowledge—that you may be filled to the measure of all the fullness of God.
>
> Now to him who is able to do immeasurably more than all we ask or imagine, according to his power that is at work within us, to him be glory in the church and in Christ Jesus throughout all generations, for ever and ever! Amen.

These very words have been prayed over you. Let this day be a new beginning of ever-deepening intimacy in your Father/daughter relationship.

# In His Arms

What is your favorite description of comfort?

- A cup of hot cocoa
- A crackling fire
- A beautiful quilt
- A warm hug
- A well-used pair of pajamas and slippers
- A familiar scent
- Cradling a special pet
- Other _____

The descriptions in this list convey a sense of warmth and familiarity, a place of safety and rest. Consider how it would feel to be drawn so close to Abba's side that you breathe in the warmth of His presence as He envelops you with His comfort. What happens in your heart as you sit quietly and imagine this scene?

# Ponder Scripture

Ashley, a brand-new child of God, faced unexpected heartbreak. She arrived home one evening to find the locks changed. Her family made it clear in this and a multitude of ways that she was no longer welcome. She felt discarded because she chose to believe.

Ashley worked hard but felt desperate most of the time. She found herself continually playing catch-up in her fight for survival. She described the paralyzing fear that cloaked her spirit each night as she fell into bed exhausted but unable to sleep. It was as if rest was held at arm's length. As we discussed Abba's caring presence, she regained some hope. By praying through one of the psalms, Ashley discovered the amazing faithfulness and comfort of her heavenly Father. She reported clinging to God's Word at night. She clutched it to her heart like a teddy bear and was able to get much-needed sleep once again.

Rather than a distant father who locks us away from him, our Abba Father is described in 2 Corinthians 1:3 as "the Father of compassion and the God of all comfort." *Robertson's Word Pictures of the New Testament* says, "He is the God of all comfort (*paraklhsew*, old word from *parakalew*, to call to one's side)," and adds, "The English word comfort is from the Latin *confortis* (brave together)."[1] Our Abba Father calls us to face life at His side knowing that in being brave together with Him, there is nothing lacking.

Paraphrase 2 Corinthians 1:3. What examples of a comforting presence in the midst of the journey have you witnessed?

Today God provided an outline of consolation when I least expected it. My faithful dog, Shadow, passed away at almost thirteen years of age. Tears flowed as I recalled the many ways God had used him as an example of what it looks like to be present with another. Shadow was a fierce and constant companion and lived up to his name. He seemed to possess a special ability to sense when I was hurting. Through some of the most agonizing moments in my life, he rested his head against my leg, nuzzled my hand, and gazed up adoringly. It was as if he were saying, "You are not alone—I care," and somehow my burden was lightened. Today, as he slipped away from me, I tried to return that same sentiment, sitting with him, stroking him, and hoping to console him. In a much more remarkable way, my Abba Father extends Himself and is present with me through the good and the bad moments of life.

Jot down a list of some emotional, relational, family, or physical challenges you are currently facing.

Ask your Abba Father to be present with you in the midst of each situation, to hold you, and to help you receive His compassion and comfort. Don't worry if you don't feel anything immediately; ask God for the grace to anticipate His goodness.

It seems logical to seek comfort when we're hurting at the hands of others, but can we turn to Abba when we are tempted or think we've already blown it?

When you think about being held in your Father's arms *just as you are*, what do you do?

- Stay there but squirm and wiggle a bit
- Resist the embrace
- Lay your head on His shoulder and relax
- Stay but with tension in your body

- Cuddle and soak up the warmth
- Snuggle up tentatively, fearing He'll change His mind
- Other _____

A college professor once suggested we draw a picture of how we see ourselves with God. Please take a moment to do a variation of that exercise. Find a blank piece of paper or some space in your journal for a few drawings. They can be as simple as stick figures or as elaborate as you wish. First draw a picture representing you and your heavenly Father. Now imagine for a moment that you are hurting because you know you have sinned; draw another picture of yourself with Abba at this moment.

Compare your drawings with the following scriptures from *The Message*:

> If your heart is broken, you'll find GOD right there;
> if you're kicked in the gut, he'll help you catch your breath.
>
> Disciples so often get into trouble;
> still, GOD is there every time. (Psalm 34:18-19)
>
> God is sheer mercy and grace;
>     not easily angered, he's rich in love.
> He doesn't endlessly nag and scold,
>     nor hold grudges forever.
> He doesn't treat us as our sins deserve,
>     nor pay us back in full for our wrongs.
> As high as heaven is over the earth,
>     so strong is his love to those who fear him.
> And as far as sunrise is from sunset,
>     he as separated us from our sins. (Psalm 103:8-12)

A Message from the high and towering God,
　　who lives in Eternity,
　　whose name is Holy:
"I live in the high and holy places,
　　but also with the low-spirited, the spirit-crushed,
And what I do is put new spirit in them,
　　get them up and on their feet again." (Isaiah 57:15)

On the other hand, if we admit our sins — make a clean
breast of them — he won't let us down; he'll be true to himself. He'll forgive our sins and purge us of all wrongdoing.
(1 John 1:9)

How does God describe His posture toward you when you are
broken?

I remember a day I experimented in practicing the presence of God.
My resolution came after reading about the monk Brother Lawrence,
who wrote of his life with God in a powerful book called *Practicing the
Presence of God*. My experiment involved seeking to live for twenty-four
hours doing everything for the love of God and acknowledging His
nearness. I launched into my venture with a nagging fear in the back
of my mind: *What if I fail? Then what?* Of course I did fail, but to my
surprise there were no finger-shaking accusations. Instead, it was as if I
were a child who'd fallen and skinned my knees. I sensed compassion,
not condemnation, as He scooped me up, cleansed me, and covered me
with a bandage of unfailing love. My gracious Father showed Himself
as a God of compassion: present, able, and willing to revive and heal,
not crush.

You might be thinking, *This all sounds good but braving life together implies trust. I don't know if I can attach that kind of trust to a father.* Brooke would agree. Her experience taught her that she couldn't trust her father to show up when he said he would. How on earth could she trust him to be there facing life with her? As a little girl, Brooke ached to see her daddy. He called and set up a time to visit. She beamed with anticipation, and when the big day came, she was ready well ahead of time. All dressed up with her hair in a pretty bow, she sat on the front steps watching for him. The time of his arrival came and went, and still she sat there refusing to believe he would stand her up. When the day passed without even a phone call, she tucked her hurt deep inside and tried to pretend it didn't matter. This whole scene replayed itself again and again. She continued to hope he would come for her, and each time he didn't, a little piece of her died. A deep sense of rejection and mistrust gradually seeped into the depths of her soul. Later on, the idea of trusting any man, even God, seemed ludicrous.

Note some of the times you've felt forsaken or ways you may have been conditioned to mistrust. On the flip side, hold in your mind a picture of someone you trust the most. What makes that person trustworthy?

What do the following scriptures tell you about the trustworthiness of your heavenly Father? Note any words or phrases that stand out to you.

- Numbers 23:19
- Psalm 27:10
- Psalm 28:7
- Psalm 36:5

- Psalm 77:10-13
- Psalm 111:7
- Psalm 145:8-18
- Lamentations 3:22-25
- Hebrews 6:17-18
- Hebrews 13:5

From these verses and verses from previous weeks, what kind of a picture of your Father's character is being formed?

On the left side of the following chart, list any trust builders God has put in your life. You can incorporate Scriptures, people, answered prayers, specific events, or ways God has revealed Himself in your life. You can also include any insights you glean from the previous verses about trustworthiness. On the right side, list some of the mysteries in your life, including things you don't understand, painful events, and prayers not yet answered.

| Trust Builders | Mysteries |
|---|---|
|  |  |
|  |  |
|  |  |
|  |  |
|  |  |
|  |  |

|  |  |
|---|---|
|  |  |
|  |  |
|  |  |
|  |  |

Ask your heavenly Father to provide you with the trust builders you need in your life to help you leave the mysteries in His hands.

Reflect on Proverbs 3:5-6:

Trust God from the bottom of your heart;
    don't try to figure out everything on your own.
Listen for God's voice in everything you do, everywhere you go;
    he's the one who will keep you on track. (MSG)

When you read these words, how do you respond?

- "Yes, God," with a nagging sense of fear.
- "I'll try God, but I really need to understand first."
- "I'm on my way to complete trust."
- "I don't need to figure anything out; I trust You implicitly."
- "Sorry, God; I want to trust, but it's hard for me."
- Other _____

Corrie ten Boom, who later in her life endured horrors at the hands of Nazis, told of a time when she was concerned that she would lack what she needed to face death. She said,

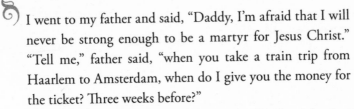

I went to my father and said, "Daddy, I'm afraid that I will never be strong enough to be a martyr for Jesus Christ." "Tell me," father said, "when you take a train trip from Haarlem to Amsterdam, when do I give you the money for the ticket? Three weeks before?"

"No, Daddy, you give me the money for the ticket just before we get on the train." "That is right," my father said, "and so it is with God's strength. Our wise Father in heaven knows when you are going to need things too."[2]

What in your life do you need to trust to the wisdom of your "wise Father in heaven"?

Our Father knows our deepest need and the fragile nature of our spirits. Regardless of our source of distress, we are restored as we flee to the quiet strength of His loving arms. Our Father knows the perfect way to cradle us. The question is, will we trust Him to hold us even in the midst of the mysteries?

### A Step of Faith
In the movie *Indiana Jones and the Last Crusade*, there is a scene where Indy is standing on a rock ledge with a huge chasm opening up before him. In order for him to continue on his journey, he must take a step of faith. When he takes that step, he sees the rock that provides a bridge.

Imagine you are standing at the edge of a "rocky cliff" in your life. Will you take a step of faith and open your heart to the comforting touch of Abba? If you were Steven Spielberg, what scene would you write to describe that step of faith in your daily life?

Go back over Proverbs 3:5-6. Form the passage into a personal prayer like the example that follows. Pray each word deliberately and out loud.

> *God, help me to trust You from the bottom of my heart; help me to leave all things in Your hands knowing I'm not to try to figure everything out on my own. I want to listen for Your voice in everything I do, everywhere I go; help me live believing that You are the one who will keep me on track.*

Now go back through the prayer and pause after each phrase, pouring out any details of your life that come to mind. Cry out to Abba. He is the God of all comfort and compassion.

## Reflect

How awesome that the Father who extends us comfort in His arms is also the glorious God of strength and majesty. He is powerful beyond comprehension, yet tender and personal. Turn to Deuteronomy 33:26-27 and make note of the images that describe God's divine care.

Not long ago, I stumbled upon a scene that could have been an illustration drawn for these verses. I worked in a children's ministry and our program for the evening was over. A sense of energy blended with exhaustion as parents mingled with children and volunteers. In the midst of her exuberant activities, a beautiful little girl fell down. She seemed stunned for only a moment. Then she flew past me and, with a tear-streaked face and her arms extended, hurled herself into a tall man's arms, crying, "Papa, Papa." With soft words of comfort, he caught her in his arms and held her while she showed him her "owie." Her earnest heart received the comfort and love of the one person in the room she knew was big and kind enough to handle her hurt.

Are there any "owies" you need to bring to your Abba Father? Imagine yourself running and crying out, "Papa, Papa," and then launching yourself into His arms. Show Him your hurts and allow the warmth of His comfort to cradle your spirit and quiet your heart. Linger there in His everlasting arms.

# Respond

It is often difficult to enter back into the frenzy of everyday living after spending intimate time with the Father. One possible way to make the transition and to keep our hearts covered in comfort is to engage in a type of prayer called "breath prayer." In her description of this practice, Adele Calhoun said, "Breath prayer reminds us that just as we can't live on one breath of air, we can't live on one breath of God. God is the oxygen of our soul, and we need to breathe him in all day long."[3] As we seek to make prayer as natural as breathing, we are drawn into the arms of Abba throughout the day. Begin by sitting comfortably and quietly. In the stillness, notice your breathing. Become aware of each time you inhale and exhale. Next allow your breathing to become the rhythm of a prayer. For example, as you breathe in, say, "Abba," and as you breathe out, say, "Hold me."

Other breath prayers could include:

- "Abba, I love You."
- "Abba, help me trust."
- "Abba, comfort me."
- "Father, heal my heart."
- "Father, remind me of Your presence."
- "Abba, be with me."
- "Abba, show me Your heart."
- "Father, have mercy on me."
- "Father, melt my heart."
- "Father, forgive my tendency to doubt You."

Quietly repeat the prayer and then be silent for a few minutes.

Write the words of your prayer where you will notice them today. As you go through your day—when you are sitting in traffic, eating lunch, or wherever you may have some kind of pause—repeat your breath prayer. As you fall asleep tonight, breathe your prayer. Try continuing this pattern for the rest of the week, altering your breath prayers each day if you wish.

# Under His Wings

Recently, I heard a pastor tell the story of a couple hoping to teach their young child his address and provide him with an awareness of his surroundings. The father wanted to create a teachable moment, so he took his son for a long walk, presumably with many twists and turns. When they were several blocks from home, the dad bent down, looked his child in the eye, and asked, "Do you know where you are and how to get home?" The child nonchalantly shook his head from side to side. Concerned, the dad said, "If you don't know where you are, then you are lost." The little boy didn't even blink an eye. He responded that even if he didn't know where he was, he still wasn't lost or afraid because his dad was with him.

In what ways has your sense of being lost evaporated as you've spent time getting to know your Abba Father? Sit quietly and consider any of the ways you have recently opened yourself to the fathering of God. What places are beginning to open but need more light and space? Offer those places to God by praying through the following words from John Baillie's *A Diary of Private Prayer*:

Almighty and most merciful Father, whose power and whose love eternally work together for the protection of Thy children, give me grace this day to put my trust in Thee.[1]

# Ponder Scripture

A number of TV news stations reported on a new type of home party, calling it the Tupperware Party of 2007. At these parties, women shared snacks and learned about using a Taser for protection.[2] If you could Taser one thing that regularly assails your heart, what would it be?

Throughout His Word, our heavenly Father is described as a shield, shelter, defender, strong tower, fortress, refuge, and hiding place. He is the ultimate protector of our lives.

Recite Psalm 91 aloud:

> He who dwells in the shelter of the Most High
>> will rest in the shadow of the Almighty.
> I will say of the LORD, "He is my refuge and my fortress,
>> my God, in whom I trust."
>
> Surely he will save you from the fowler's snare
>> and from the deadly pestilence.
> He will cover you with his feathers,
>> and under his wings you will find refuge;
>> his faithfulness will be your shield and rampart.
> You will not fear the terror of night,
>> nor the arrow that flies by day,
> nor the pestilence that stalks in the darkness,
>> nor the plague that destroys at midday.
> A thousand may fall at your side,
>> ten thousand at your right hand,
>> but it will not come near you.
> You will only observe with your eyes
>> and see the punishment of the wicked.

If you make the Most High your dwelling—
>even the LORD, who is my refuge—
then no harm will befall you,
>no disaster will come near your tent.
For he will command his angels concerning you
>to guard you in all your ways;
they will lift you up in their hands,
>so that you will not strike your foot against a stone.
You will tread upon the lion and the cobra;
>you will trample the great lion and the serpent.

"Because he loves me," says the LORD, "I will rescue him;
>I will protect him, for he acknowledges my name.
He will call upon me, and I will answer him;
>I will be with him in trouble,
>I will deliver him and honor him,
With long life will I satisfy him
>and show him my salvation."

Go back through this psalm and underline the phrases that describe what we do and circle the ones that describe what God's does. What do the words depicting God's actions tell you about His heart toward you?

This psalm speaks of terrors, plagues, predators, and disasters that can come against us. What disasters are coming near your tent, your dwelling place? Where is your heart most vulnerable?

The psalmist writes of rest and refuge in the midst of circumstances that would send most of us screaming in terror. He trusts himself to the covering of his God and at one point uses the beautiful image of being covered by feathers and hidden under wings. How good of our Father to speak to us in images from nature that we can see and take into our heart. A bird's feathers provide protection from the sunlight, wind, rain, and predators. They insulate, providing warmth and safety for baby birds.

Pretend you are an illustrator and draw a picture that represents what we read in Psalm 91. Include the dangers that confront your heart. If the idea of drawing intimidates you, list the threats to your heart and then cover them with feathery strokes of a pen or pencil.

Throughout the week, take advantage of any opportunities to do some bird watching. Marvel at the construction of a bird's feathers. Let your imagination go and think about being hidden under their wings.

Psalm 63:7 says, "Because you are my help, I sing in the shadow of your wings." As you intentionally seek to rest in the warmth and safety your tender Father provides, sing in the shadow of His wings. What song will you sing? Some ideas include "He Knows My Name," "Oh No You Never Let Go," and "There Is a Place of Quiet Rest," or you can simply hum your favorite melody or worship song.

## Protective Boundaries

When you come across a fence or boundary of some type, is your gut reaction positive or negative? Do you see restriction or safety?

When you were a child, what kind of boundaries did your earthly father set for you?

- None
- Harsh
- Legalistic
- Reassuring
- Other _____

What happened if you violated the rules?

## Boundary Tales

Terry walked in fear of rules. Her parents established boundaries that seemed harsh, unreasonable, and often arbitrary, yet she could not stand up against them for fear of physical revenge. She became timid, working harder than anyone else to prove she kept the rules and trying to avoid punishment. To her, boundaries seem more like threats and excuses for torment.

Sandy admits to mixed reactions to boundaries. She smiles compliantly but inwardly sneers. She has this desire to ignore the fence and show that it won't stop her.

Lisa hears jokes about overprotective fathers and laughs along with everyone else to hide the pain of feeling exposed, but secretly she envies girls with protective fathers.

Jody hears flippant remarks like "Go play in traffic" and also laughs along with others, yet for her, dangerous exploration really was a way of life. There was a time she wished for boundaries of any kind. Friends seemed to envy her apparent freedom; no one set limits on her behavior, for the most part. Jody never would have admitted to them that her "freedom" was counterfeit.

Samantha felt lured into a darkness that ate away at her soul bit by bit. She ventured beyond the fences, wondering all the while if anyone cared. Did anyone bigger and wiser even exist? She became promiscuous and went "looking for love in all the wrong places." Yet lurking beneath her behavior was a sad little girl who questioned why no one was concerned enough to place boundaries on her behavior.

Do you identify with any of these women? In what way?

Explore Psalm 16. What do *you* think is God's motivation for establishing boundaries?

Verse 6 says, "The boundary lines have fallen for me in *pleasant places*" (emphasis added). Can you think of an example of a pleasant boundary?

Our Abba Father knows us inside and out. He knows what will bring death and what will bring life. He doesn't saddle us with a list of legalistic rules designed to weigh us down, hover like a vulture, and then mete out harsh punishment the moment He catches us disobeying. Instead, He provides principles for life—full, abundant, and boundless life. As we choose to trust the wisdom of the boundaries He sets, knowing He values us enough to give true freedom, we take our first steps toward embracing an unchained obedience. We learn to walk in safety and guard our hearts. He provides spacious dwelling places where we breathe the air of life, yet He still grants us the opportunity to choose where we will reside daily.

While reading Colossians 3:1-17, consider some of the boundaries God places on your life. Draw a heart in the following space and then list the boundaries. Inside the heart, place life-giving boundaries; outside of it, place those that bring death to your spirit.

Now read Ephesians 5:1-20 and add to the heart any additional boundaries. Which relationships in your life would be most affected if you regularly honored those boundaries?

- Romantic
- Family
- Coworkers
- Friends
- Other _____

Choose one relationship that stands out to you and lay it before the Lord in prayer. Ask Him for specific ways to live within the safety of His design for your heart. If you need a time of confession and restoration, try making Psalm 32 a personal prayer. Note that this psalm ends with rejoicing and singing. Is there a way you can celebrate Abba's protective boundaries?

Another dimension of Abba's protective care involves empowering us to set personal limits with others in our lives. So often we equate limits with selfishness or we aren't sure "when to say yes" and "when to say no."[3] Some of us were not instructed on how to determine what makes a limit appropriate. "Boundaries help us keep the good in and the bad out."[4] I spent years feeling guilty when I was not meeting the needs of all the people in my life. I churned up valuable energy engaging in an internal tug-of-war. Taking time to learn what I am and am not responsible for has helped me guard my heart. My heavenly Father knows my struggle and continually sets before me resources for growth. He's birthed a restful sanctuary within my heart where I live shielded from the harsh demands of myself and others. If this is an area you sense God calling you to examine, I highly recommend Dr. Henry Cloud and Dr. John Townsend's book *Boundaries* or a support group working together on this concept.

## A Final Word About Boundaries

Sometimes boundaries are crossed in such violent ways that we need intensive care.

Cindi shared her dilemma in learning to apply appropriate boundaries in her life. A close male family member, who should have been protective, violated Cindi's sexual boundaries. Again and again, she was subjected to horrific violations of her body, and those she told about it didn't believe her. The very people she counted on for protection assailed her.

If you share Cindi's pain in some way, I am truly sorry for what you have endured, and I grieve with you. May you be bathed in Abba's warmth and rest safely in His arms. May His love soothe and heal your brokenness.

Taking steps of healing can feel like trudging through a swamp where the mud impairs movement and the mess clings to your heart. Please allow someone to walk with you in your pain. Abba sometimes provides for us by gifting others to take our hand and help us walk, hose off the mud, and guide us to freedom. Please don't hesitate to attend to the cries of your heart and allow someone to walk with you in your pain.

# Reflect

When Abby was a little girl, she longed to step off the school bus and know she was coming home to a place of safety. She wanted a safe niche—not an escape but a very real shelter from the storms of life. Abby wished she could bring every fear, hurt, and trouble to someone bigger and stronger, someone who could draw her into the security of his arms. Then sitting there, she could fully relax. Now she knows she is a child of the Most High and she runs to her Abba. When she's afraid, when life is overwhelming, Abby runs home to her Abba Father and rests in the shadow of His wings. Now she prays along with the psalmist, "You are my hiding place; you will protect me from trouble and surround me with songs of deliverance" (32:7).

Consider the following excerpt from *The Christian's Secret of a Happy Life*:

> Do you recollect the delicious sense of rest with which you have sometimes gone to bed at night after a day of great exertion and weariness? . . . You trusted yourself to the bed in absolute confidence, and it held you up, without effort, or strain, or even thought, on your part. You rested!
>
> But suppose you had doubted the strength or the stability of your bed and had dreaded each moment to find it giving way beneath you and landing you on the floor; could you have rested then? Would not every muscle have been strained in a fruitless effort to hold yourself up, and would not the weariness have been greater than if you had not gone to bed at all?
>
> Let this analogy teach you what it means to rest in the Lord. Let your souls lie down upon the couch of His sweet will, as your bodies lie down in their beds at night. Relax every strain and lay off every burden. Let yourself go in a perfect abandonment of ease and comfort sure that since He holds you up, you are perfectly safe.[5]

What longings do you experience as you read this excerpt?

Read the words of Psalm 4:8: "I will lie down and sleep in peace, for you alone, O LORD, make me dwell in safety." Each night as you go to bed, recite this verse. Let Abba tuck you in for the night and rest in the security of His Word. Create a bedtime ritual with your Father, surrounding yourself with His love. What will you include? Does He tell you the story of His love for you and pull the covers up under your chin before kissing you good night? Revel in Abba's tender loving care as you fall asleep.

# Respond

You are a daughter of a King. May you have your identity as Abba's girl eternally imprinted on your heart. For the next week, imagine that everywhere you go, every time you enter a room, the words "Daughter of the Most High King" are tattooed on your forehead. Place a sticker, temporary tattoo, or other symbol near your mirror and in your car to remind you of this exercise. Journal throughout the week about any changes in your days.

Conclude your study this week with the following prayer from Thomas à Kempis:

Write thy blessed name, O Lord, upon my heart, there to remain so indelibly engraven, that no prosperity, no adversity shall ever move me from thy love. Be thou to me a strong tower of defence, a comforter in tribulation, a deliverer in distress, a very present help in trouble, and a guide to heaven through the many temptations and dangers of this life. Amen.[6]

# Through Abba's Eyes

In the movie *Shrek*, an ogre becomes Princess Fiona's knight in shining armor who rescues her from a fire-breathing dragon. His intention is to take her to the king. At first Fiona resembles the classic image of a beautiful princess with a few unusual quirks, but at night her appearance changes. Princess Fiona describes herself as "beautiful by day and hideous by night."[1] Shrek doesn't see her in the same way. He turns the image upside down and finds her most beautiful at night.

Do you think beauty is in the eye of the beholder? Describe something or someone beautiful. What makes that person beautiful?

A group of people were recently asked to think of the most beautiful woman they knew. Without consulting each other, they didn't pick a glamorous celebrity. All of them picked women they know who were much older and very wise. All the women chosen had gray hair![2]

What do you think the reasons were for these women's choices?

## Ponder Scripture

Insert your name in the following sentence: "_____ is a beautiful work crafted by her Father's hands."

How does your heart respond to that statement? What questions arise?

I have a coffee-table book called *The Art of God* displayed where I have regular access to the amazing art inside. The images are a feast for the eyes and soul. Each picture is intended to inspire us to "look at the splendor of God's creation through new eyes and praise Him for the great things He has done."[3] Each wonder of nature photographed is beautiful, yet the special way God created each of us is equally amazing.

We are His workmanship (see Ephesians 2:10) made by His own hands and brought to life by His very breath (see Genesis 2:7). The word *workmanship* might sound a little sterile; however, as Jersuha Clark reminds us, the Greek word used in the Ephesians text is *poiema*, "from which we get our English word *poem*. Poetry is not a crude art form; rather, it takes tremendous skill and precision to craft a poem well. . . . As His poemia, you are a glorious masterpiece."[4]

Sit quietly for a few minutes and ask your Father to hold you in His lap as you read Psalm 139:13-16 in *The Message*, keeping in mind that it is a personal portrayal of you:

> You shaped me first inside, then out;
>     you formed me in my mother's womb.
> I thank you, High God—you're breathtaking!
>     Body and soul, I am marvelously made!
>     I worship in adoration—what a creation!
> You know me inside and out,
>     you know every bone in my body;
> You know exactly how I was made, bit by bit,
>     how I was sculpted from nothing into something.
> Like an open book, you watched me grow from conception to
>         birth;
>     all the stages of my life were spread out before you,
> The days of my life all prepared
>     before I'd even lived one day.

Notice there is nothing about you that surprises God. He isn't shocked by the shape of your nose, the sound of your voice, or the texture of your hair. He knows *every* detail there is to know about you and sees you as "marvelously made" (verse 14, MSG).

Now purposefully read each word aloud and repeat the added refrain as if you are participating in a responsive reading:

> You shaped me first inside, then out;
>     you formed me in my mother's womb.
> I thank you, High God—you're breathtaking!
>     Body and soul, I am marvelously made!
>     I worship in adoration—what a creation!

**Refrain:** You shaped me first inside, then out;
I thank you, High God—you're breathtaking!

You know me inside and out,
        you know every bone in my body;
You know exactly how I was made, bit by bit,
        how I was sculpted from nothing into something.

**Refrain:** You shaped me first inside, then out;
I thank you, High God—you're breathtaking!

Like an open book, you watched me grow from conception
            to birth;
        all the stages of my life were spread out before you,
The days of my life all prepared
        before I'd even lived one day.

**Refrain:** You shaped me first inside, then out;
I thank you, High God—you're breathtaking!

## Seeing Yourself Through Abba's Eyes

What did you see in your earthly dad's eyes when he looked at you? What words, if any, did he use to describe you? If you are one of the many women who has never met your father, what do you wish he would say if he ever lays eyes upon your face?

In 1 Samuel 16:7, we are told, "The Lord does not look at the things man looks at. Man looks at the outward appearance, but the Lord looks at the heart." I've found that verse both comforting and convicting. It's good to know that my Father "gets me" and really sees what I feel, hope for, and care about. I know He also sees the stuff I'd like to hide from Him and everyone else.

In the movie *The Devil Wears Prada*, Meryl Streep plays a ruthless woman whose appraising eye finds fashion flaws in her employees' dress. She's harsh, cold, and unrelenting in her criticism. The people around her respond frantically, scurrying around to appease her demands as if they're tossing food to a stalking tiger. There was a time when my image of God didn't differ much from Streep's character. The idea of escaping swift judgment seemed futile. But as I've grown to know Abba, I've learned He doesn't show me my sin to shame me into despair; His goal is redemption. He cleanses me, forms me, and gives life. He is an expert artist shaping me. Sometimes I can almost feel His hands molding me, reassuring me that although He sees all of me, I'm loved and touchable.

Imagine that you are sitting still, aware of Abba's eyes on you as His hands are engaged in a hands-on and personal forming of all that you are. What sensations are you aware of? Is it hard to keep from cringing? Do you see tenderness in His gaze?

Try writing a prayer to your Father expressing any fears or sense of wonder. Ask Him for the ability to receive His loving gaze.

## Abba's Beautiful Girl

Jessie shared a positive story that helped me picture the impact of a healthy connection between a father and daughter. Her face lit up as she shared why she was waiting to experience sexual intimacy on her wedding night. Jessie told how her daddy communicated his vision of her value in thousands of ways. Hugs were always available, and under his watchful eye she blossomed, accepting her uniqueness as beautiful and precious. As Jessie spoke, I stood in awe of the transforming power of a daddy's eyes. It was like the veil parted for a moment and I caught a glimpse of Abba's eyes. We are His girls. We belong to Him. He looks at us and sees a cherished masterpiece.

We are born valuable, created in the image of God. The day we are reborn in Christ and become Abba's girls, we are given an even deeper beauty.

Read the following scriptures and recount some of the beautiful characteristics of one who is "in Christ."

| Scripture Passage | Characteristics |
|---|---|
| Isaiah 61:10 | |
| Ezekiel 36:25-27 | |
| Romans 8:1 | |
| 1 Corinthians 6:11 | |
| 2 Corinthians 5:16-17 | |
| Galatians 5:22-23 | |

| Ephesians 1:3-7 | |
|---|---|
| Ephesians 2:10 | |
| Ephesians 2:13 | |
| Ephesians 2:22 | |
| Ephesians 4:24 | |
| Colossians 2:10 | |

When Abba looks at you, He sees one who is in Christ. He sees potential, uniqueness, treasure, and beauty. His eyes glow with tenderness and love as He fixes His gaze upon you.

Filmmaker Federico Fellini said, "Our minds can shape the way a thing will be because we act according to our expectations."[5] What would change the most in your daily life if you were mindful of how Abba sees you?

- Relationships with men
- Time spent comparing yourself to others
- Internal dialogue about appearance
- Self-talk about something else
- Other _____

Consider picking a verse from the table above and memorizing it. Post it where you will see it often. Ask God to make it sink into the marrow of your soul and transform you.

## Just Like Daddy

Have you ever oohed and aahed over a new baby and said something like, "Oh, she's beautiful; she looks just like her dad." As I was reflecting on the wonder of relating to Abba with tender intimacy, the knowledge that He is my perfect Daddy, I was turned inside out by these thoughts: *What would it be like to be told I resemble my heavenly Father? How would it feel for my face to become a visual reminder for others of His face?* Then I realized the opportunity to increasingly reflect Him is my honor and privilege.

Read 2 Corinthians 3:16-18. In these verses, you see that not only did He plan to adopt you, He also planned for your transformation. You were chosen to reflect His beauty, chosen to be conformed to His likeness. Imagine that you are hidden behind a veil, even grab a piece of fabric or paper, and slowly act out this passage. With each lowering of the veil, no matter how miniscule, a little more of your face is exposed.

As we seek to know God and live as His child, a little more of His face is revealed. Even in the seemingly insignificant moments of our days, we can seek to be more like Him.

There's a commercial I rarely ignore even though I've seen it over and over. I'm not sure what product is being advertised, as that's not what draws me in. The little girl and her daddy capture my attention. The dad is eating a peanut butter sandwich with his daughter. She watches him fold his bread over before eating and ultimately sits at his side and imitates him. There's gentle cuddling and an exchanged smile as the dad accepts and enjoys the little girl's adoration in her imitation.

Mull over Ephesians 5:1-2: "Be imitators of God, therefore, as dearly loved children and live a life of love, just as Christ loved us and gave himself up for us as a fragrant offering and sacrifice to God."

Now read the same passage from *The Message*:

> Watch what God does, and then you do it, like children
> who learn proper behavior from their parents. Mostly what
> God does is love you. Keep company with him and learn
> a life of love. Observe how Christ loved us. His love was

not cautious but extravagant. He didn't love in order to get something from us but to give everything of himself to us. Love like that.

What prompts the imitation? What kind of life reflects the Father? Jot down any other details you notice.

Try forming this scripture into a personal prayer. If this is difficult right now, try praying something like this:

> *Abba Father, I'm so grateful that You dearly love me. I'm thankful You have made me Your very own. Teach me to stay close by and watch You. I want to imitate You. I'm so glad to be identified as one who is in Christ. Fill me with Your amazing love for others. Empower me to live a poured-out life like Jesus as I overflow with love for You and others. May my life proclaim from the rooftops, "I am Abba's girl!" Display Your glory through me. Amen.*

Think about the commercial I mentioned that features the little girl imitating her dad. How might your day change if you focused on being just like Abba and receiving His smile? Make a game of logging as many "peanut butter–eating moments" as you can and then journal any insights from the day. As those moments increase, so does our eternal beauty.

Beauty tips are common in women's magazines. There are so many women's magazines, and most of them regularly provide detailed instructions on what to include in our morning and evening routine to improve our looks. Audrey Hepburn had a favorite list of beauty tips, from a poem written by Sam Levenson for his grandchild.

> For attractive lips, speak words of kindness.
> For lovely eyes, seek out the good in people.
> For a slim figure, share your food with the hungry.
> For beautiful hair, let a child run his or her fingers through it once a day.
> For poise, walk with the knowledge you'll never walk alone.
> People, even more than things, have to be restored, renewed, revived, reclaimed and redeemed;
> Never throw out anybody.[6]

Choose one of the following experiments to try:

- If you were asked to share beauty tips for Abba's girls, what would you include?
- Pretend you're writing a magazine column about establishing morning and evening beauty routines designed to bring out the characteristics of the Father. What practices would you suggest?
- Create a mirror that reflects your beauty in the eyes of your Father. You could use a song, a painting, an actual mirror, a list of Scripture, and so on. Be as creative and imaginative as you wish.
- Use lipstick or dry erase marker to write beauty tips on your mirror and review them each day.

Memorize these words from Psalm 45:11: "The king is enthralled by your beauty; honor him, for he is your lord." Then pray,

> *Father, I can hardly believe that You are enthralled*
> *by my beauty. What a wonderful thought! Clothe*
> *me with the beauty of a life that honors You. When*

*I entertain negative thoughts about my appearance
or have a bad-hair day, remind me of the eternal
beauty You've bestowed upon me. Teach me to live
each day with dignity and to see myself as Your
precious child. Amen.*

# Reflect

You are in Christ. You are a daughter of the King. You are crowned with beauty, adorned with praise, and a new creation displaying the amazing love of your Father.

Read Isaiah 61:3. Let the next few moments become holy ground. Do something ceremonial to mark the moment, such as lighting a candle or going to a special place outdoors.

Fall to your knees before Abba and imagine all the ashes of your life swept away. As you bow before your Father, imagine a crown of beauty placed on your head. Feel it settle in on your hair and consider how you are defined by this crown of beauty now. Let the oil of gladness wash over you and receive the garment of praise. Let your aching spirit be immersed in life and cloaked in joy. Say out loud, "I am Your daughter, Abba Father, crowned, anointed, clothed, and eternally displayed as Your cherished work of art."

In your journal, give a description of your coronation ceremony reflecting on one or two of the following questions:

- What specifically was swept away?
- How does it feel to be drenched with oil of gladness?
- What happens to your face when you are clothed with praise and crowned with beauty?
- What is taken on as you arise? What is different about you?
- How might you carry this moment with you from this point on?

# Respond

This week, pretend you are a photographer and thoughtfully choose what you want to capture on film. Some possible subjects may be a tree, a flower, a leaf, a rock, running water, or a person. Take several pictures and reflect on how you chose to frame the view. How do you think Abba frames you? What if He planned a photo exhibit of His favorite pictures of you? What would be included? What action shots would be captured? What X-ray views? What happens in your heart when you think about Abba treasuring you, His masterpiece?

Pray one more time through the responsive reading based on Psalm 139 (MSG):

> You shaped me first inside, then out;
>> you formed me in my mother's womb.
> I thank you, High God—you're breathtaking!
>> Body and soul, I am marvelously made!
>> I worship in adoration—what a creation!

> **Refrain:** You shaped me first inside, then out;
> I thank you, High God—you're breathtaking!

> You know me inside and out,
>> you know every bone in my body;
> You know exactly how I was made, bit by bit,
>> how I was sculpted from nothing into something.

> **Refrain:** You shaped me first inside, then out;
> I thank you, High God—you're breathtaking!

> Like an open book, you watched me grow from conception
>> to birth;

all the stages of my life were spread out before you,
The days of my life all prepared
    before I'd even lived one day.

**Refrain:** You shaped me first inside, then out;
I thank you, High God—you're breathtaking!

# A Generous Father

Last Christmas I tore into a long tubular package with curious gusto. My mom had created a lot of anticipation by expressing how much she wished she could see my face as I opened it. The package lived up to its mystery, and then some. With great delight, I uncovered a one-of-a-kind theater poster featuring my twin sons. Later I learned that my mom had delivered photos, an old program from the production, and any information she could find to a printer to have this gift made to order just for me. Knowing that this gift was birthed in my mom's heart made it a priceless treasure.

When was the last time you searched for that perfect gift for someone special? With that occasion in mind, consider the following questions:

- What motivated you to devote time and effort to selecting this gift?
- How did you wrap it?
- What did you imagine as you anticipated the moment it would be opened?
- What happened in your heart as you watched that person receive your gift?

◆ What comes to mind when you hear that your Abba Father delights in lavishing priceless gifts on you?

## Ponder Scripture

Turn to Matthew 7:7-11 and Luke 11:9-13 and read them aloud. What images or words come to mind?

- ◆ A coiling and hissing serpent
- ◆ A scorpion
- ◆ Bread snatched away
- ◆ A gift tied up with a bow
- ◆ Hands outstretched to give
- ◆ Open hands to receive
- ◆ Other _____

### Spiders and Snakes

Patricia Zimmerman, in her book *My Father Gave Me a Serpent*, chronicles her struggle with Matthew 7:7-11. For years, she believed that her father did give her a serpent—in the shape of a legacy of alcoholism, abuse, and pain.[1] Mary Jane, played by Kirsten Dunst in the *Spider-Man* movies, received spiders and snakes too. We get glimpses of Mary Jane's harsh home life and hear her drunken father shouting obscenities. In *Spider-Man 3*, she confides to Peter Parker (aka Spider-Man) how the words of her father were like poison, dooming her to never amount to anything.

What have you unwrapped over the years from your earthly father? Take a moment to make a list of both the positives and negatives.

If the disappointments on your list seem overwhelming, what will help you open your hands and allow your Abba Father to surprise you with His generosity?

Review Matthew 7:7-11 and Luke 11:9-13 one more time. Notice the hope in Jesus' words. He isn't saying that our heavenly Father will respond just like earthly fathers or even that all earthly fathers give good gifts. He is pouring out amazing news: Even the best of dads can't begin to match the pure generosity of the heavenly Father. One commentary puts it this way: "How much more will the heavenly Father, who is inherently perfectly holy and good, always give to his children what they need when they ask him."[2]

This week, Abba immersed me in the truth of this scripture in a fresh way. Like a fog creeping over a city before morning, my day started with medical uncertainty about my husband, Thom. Doctors told us that Thom had a tumor inside his spinal cord and a risky surgery would be necessary. I fell to my knees, begging my Father for His presence, and after a time rose with the assurance of His presence and the conviction that God would receive glory in the midst of this turmoil.

In the meantime, Abba had been planting seeds of new relationship with my earthly father. I was stunned when my dad, who in spite of some physical challenges, drove more than eight hundred miles to be with me because, as he'd said, "he couldn't do otherwise." I read Matthew 7:11 again with tears as I heard the gentle voice of my Father impressing on me, "Rita, if your dad couldn't do otherwise, how could I? I am here." My wonderful Abba Father goes to even greater lengths to be with me, to care for and comfort me, than anyone. His generous nature and goodness amaze me over and over again and draw me to rest in His loving arms.

We have a Father who gives Himself, His very presence, to His children. Imagine that the gift of a loving heavenly Father sits before you ready to be opened. How is it wrapped? As you open your gift, what is the first thing you notice? What have you been unpacking over the past weeks of this study?

## Perfect Gifts

Turn to James 1:17-18 and explore the giving heart of Abba.

Abba's heart isn't fickle. He won't abandon you, skip over you, or give you leftovers. His giving isn't accidental or haphazard. Verse 18 says that the heavenly Father "chose to give us birth." Personalize that verse by placing your name in the blank: "He chose to give _____ birth." Repeat that phrase with quiet firmness and then again as if you are announcing exciting news to the world. Savor the truth. You are a wanted child.

How does your heart respond to those words?

The gift of new birth along with "every good and perfect gift" (verse 17) falls from the fingertips of Abba to be opened and treasured by His girls. Abba loves to give. He knows everything there is to know about you, even desires not yet awakened. He sees your deepest wishes, your likes, your needs, and what delights your heart. In *The Message*, the words describing Abba's gifts are *desirable* and *beneficial*. There is nothing bad or dark mixed in; His gifts are pure goodness thoughtfully prepared for you.

> Every desirable and beneficial gift comes out of heaven. The gifts are rivers of light cascading down from the Father of Light. There is nothing deceitful in God, nothing two-faced, nothing fickle. He brought us to life using the true Word, showing us off as the crown of all his creatures. (James 1:17-18, MSG)

Search through the following Scriptures and list any gifts you find:

- Isaiah 40:29-31 _____
- Jeremiah 31:3 _____
- John 3:16 _____
- Romans 2:4 _____
- Romans 5:1 _____
- Ephesians 2:8 _____
- James 1:5 _____
- 2 Peter 1:3-4 _____

May you revel in the wonder of Abba's abounding care as we open even more of His gracious gifts. Abba's eyes are on you, enjoying the expression on your face, squeals of delight, or tears of joy as you deliberately reach for and open each package.

## The Gift of the Holy Spirit

Lara sits sipping a cup of tea, and as she sets it down, exasperation spills from every gesture and the tone of her voice. She's sharing her frustration about a guy's behavior and his tendency to come and go in her life.

One moment he's incredibly attentive and she thinks she might be his girlfriend. Then it's like he's fallen off the face of the earth and she hears absolutely nothing from him for more than a month. *Am I his girlfriend or not?* she wonders. She just wants to know exactly where she stands.

Abba doesn't leave us wondering whether or not we belong to Him. From a tender Father heart, He gives the Holy Spirit, who makes our status real and known.

Although we spent time in Romans 8 and Ephesians 1 earlier in the study, let's revisit a few specific verses. Go back over Romans 8:15-16 and Ephesians 1:13-14. Also read Galatians 4:6; John 14:16,26; and 1 John 3:24. Then note in your journal any words or phrases concerning the Holy Spirit that capture your attention.

Abba provides for us in the times when we wonder if we're really His. He doesn't keep it a secret from us but marks and seals our hearts, covering our fear with the truth that we belong to Him. When you read statements like this, which, if any, of the following things do you do?

- Say that I know this in my head but not my heart
- Become wistful
- Feel assurance
- Wish for assurance but wonder why I don't sense it immediately
- Feel left out
- Well up with tears of joy
- Other _____

Whatever your response, will you lay it before your Father now? Choose one phrase from one of the verses mentioned a few paragraphs back and make it your prayer for the next week. Ask your Father to flesh out each word for you in the coming weeks and remove anything from your heart that covers up the truth that you belong completely to Him.

Luke 11:13 is worded this way in *The Message*: "Don't you think the

Father who conceived you in love will give you the Holy Spirit when you ask him?" When was the last time you considered the wonderful gift of the Holy Spirit as falling from the fingertips of your gracious Abba Father? Take a few moments to pause and thank Him for His goodness, and then ask Him to refresh His gift of the Holy Spirit in your heart.

There are many other dimensions of the Father's gift of the Holy Spirit, so many that they are beyond the scope of this study. Still, I can't resist highlighting just one more. Recently, a repairman came to my home to look at a new piece of furniture that was defective. I was surprised when he showed up in the middle of a school day with his twelve-year-old daughter. She assisted him in the process of appraising the damage, holding his camera, and taking a picture when he asked. It was fun to watch her help her dad and participate in his work. Later I discovered it was Take Our Daughters to Work Day. I thought, *How cool is that?*

We have an even greater place alongside our Father. As Abba's daughters, we have the privilege of participating in the most amazing work of all. In this book *Desiring God's Will,* David Benner said, "God loves so much he wants to transform all people and all things by love. God wants to spread love by propagating the divine self in us and through us."[3] No equipment is lacking. He provides the power, the gifts that fit your temperament and talents, and offers you the opportunity to be used in love for His grand plan.

Read Romans 12:4-8, 1 Corinthians 12:4-11, and Ephesians 4:11-13. We are all given gifts so that we may participate in the building of God's kingdom. Ask your Father to help you recognize and use the gifts He's given you. If you're unsure of your gifts, take a spiritual gifts inventory. A pastor or another Christ follower could recommend a particular gifts assessment. Also, you could explore the possibilities on the websites of Willow Creek or Saddleback Church. Then, as you work alongside your Father, thank Him for including you and taking you to work with Him.

## More Presents

The first two chapters of Genesis describe the magnificence of creation. Close your eyes and for a few moments let your imagination run with the scene in the Garden of Eden before the Fall. What sights and sounds greet your senses? What colors would you want to see? What fragrances fill the air? Can you hear running water? What textures touch your fingertips or graze your arms as you walk in the garden? How does the fruit taste?

Abba Father formed us with the ability to see in color, to hear, to smell, to touch, and to appreciate the wonder of His creativity. He invites us to notice the details, to remember that He is the "maker of dragonflies and pussywillows."[4] He beckons us to come out and play in His presence.

If you can, spend some time at a park or recall a time at a park watching children play. Listen to their cries for attention—"Watch me, swing me"—and their squeals of delight. What happens to the faces of those whose daddies respond in love?

On a vacation, I had the opportunity to explore a rain forest on the island of Dominica. As we glided gradually through the canopy on an aerial tram, I was surrounded by the majesty of God. I was flooded with awe and could do nothing but say, "This is so beautiful, Father." Instantly I heard that still small voice answer something like this: "I'm so glad you enjoy it; I made it for you." What a giving Father! Words failed me as my heart rushed forward to thank Him.

How incredible that my Father would enjoy watching me enjoy the gift of creation, that He would notice my exhilaration as I plunge into an ocean wave or roll down a hill.

Sit outside if you can or by a window and say or sing the words of the hymn "This Is My Father's World":

> This is my Father's world
> And to my listening ear

All nature sings and round me rings the music of the spheres
This is my Father's world
I rest me in the thought
Of rocks and trees, of skies and seas
His hand the wonders wrought

As we revel in the beauty of our Father's creativity, He also gifts us with the reminder of His majesty, glory, and power. Our Abba is tender and caring. At the same time, He is awesome and able. Again, if possible, position yourself so that you can view the outside; look up to the heavens and declare aloud the words of Psalm 19:1-6. Be still before Him, allowing your heart to settle in the wonder of His amazing presence, and then worship Him with all your being. You could bow before Him, lift your hands to the heavens, or sing "How Great Thou Art," "Indescribable," "Glory in the Highest," or whatever song springs to your lips.

## You Are a Gift of the Father

No one begins to match the lavish generosity of our God. Not only is the Father your source of "every good and perfect gift" (James 1:17), He even gives you as a precious gift to Jesus.

Read John 17:24 and 10:29. What happens in your heart as you absorb the wondrous knowledge that you are given as a costly gift to Jesus?

# Reflect

In the movie *The Day After Tomorrow*, a character played by Jake Gyllenhaal is trapped by a terrible storm in a portion of the Manhattan library. He and the girl he shyly pursues are reflecting on a good day. Jake has no trouble coming up with a day he treasured. It wasn't a day of doing exciting things but a rainy day that forced focused time alone with his dad.

Abba has gone to great lengths to restore our fellowship with Him. The words of John 3:16 have been repeated so many times that we risk skimming over an awesome gift. God loves us so much that He gave the ultimate gift of becoming His beloved child forever. He wants us with Him and is never too busy to spend time with us.

Do you need some rainy-day time with Abba? Would you consider planning a time away with just Him? It could be for an hour or two, half a day, or even a full day.

Here are some suggestions for your rainy day with Him:

◆ Pray the following prayer:

> *My Father, you welcome me into your presence . . .*
> *by the blood and the word of my Lord Jesus, your*
> *Son. In this moment, in spirit, I want to be with*
> *you, sitting at your feet . . . enjoying your love . . .*
> *so that I may walk today in this thirsty and dark*
> *world and carry with me a cool drink of your*
> *presence . . . a reflection of your brightness.*[5]

◆ Take a walk with Him.
◆ Meditate on a favorite scripture or one that's been speaking to your heart.
◆ Remind yourself of His presence, even imagining that He is

right next to you, and simply enjoy His nearness.

◆ Pour out your heart, your fears, hopes, and dreams to Him.

◆ Listen quietly in His presence. Don't be concerned if the time is silent. Sometimes just being together is the best thing.

◆ Draw, sing, or journal your heart to Him.

As your rainy-day time draws to a close, bathe in the wonder of what you've been given, journal your thoughts, and thank God for time away with Him.

# Respond

As I look back over this week's focus, I realize we've made only a small dent in opening the pile of presents Abba sets before us. I pray He has empowered you to receive His gifts in faith.

Ephesians 5:20 instructs us to give "thanks to God the Father for everything." Try honoring this exhortation by writing a thank-you card to your Abba Father for His many gifts. Tuck the card into your Bible and review it occasionally, reminding yourself anew of Abba's extravagant generosity.

Please pray with me:

> *Abba Father, it seems a little like Christmas morning. I wake up surrounded by gifts. Your generous heart overwhelms me. I feel the urge to run into Your arms and say, "Thank You, thank You, thank You." I'm sorry for the times I've overlooked Your goodness. Sometimes You seem almost too good to be true. Please open my eyes to the wonder of living life as Your little girl. Help me to fully receive the gifts You give and let my whole life become an expression of loving gratitude. Amen.*

# A Daughter's Inheritance

In the book *The Art of Possibility*, Benjamin Zander shared an experiment he conducted with a class of graduate students at the New England Conservatory called "Giving the A." From the start of the class, all students were informed they would receive an A for the course.[1]

What if this happened to you? Imagine yourself as a college freshman who's feeling a bit nervous or intimidated. On the first day of class, the professor walks in, looks directly at you, and announces that you already have an A regardless of your performance in the coming weeks. How would that affect your attitude throughout the semester? Would you still feel the need to prove yourself, or would you receive the grade and enjoy it?

As a child of God, you've already been awarded more than an A based on the performance of Jesus. You've been given a rich inheritance. What's your initial response to that idea?

- ◆ I question if it's too good to be true.
- ◆ I can't wrap my mind around it.
- ◆ I think that it sounds good but doesn't seem real.
- ◆ I wonder how to claim that A.

- ◆ I feel free to grow in an atmosphere of acceptance.
- ◆ Other _____

Your eternal life began the moment you became Abba's child. Your inheritance is meant to be claimed and received. How gut-wrenching would it be to watch an orphan rummaging through a dump for nourishment while a gourmet meal topped off with a scrumptious dessert sits before her untouched? Yet, like this orphan, we sometimes live unaware of the riches of our Father's love.

Consider the following words of C. S. Lewis:

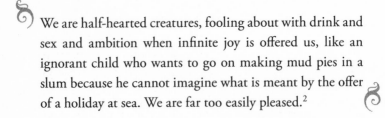

We are half-hearted creatures, fooling about with drink and sex and ambition when infinite joy is offered us, like an ignorant child who wants to go on making mud pies in a slum because he cannot imagine what is meant by the offer of a holiday at sea. We are far too easily pleased.[2]

How hard is it for you to "imagine what is meant by the offer of a holiday at sea"?

As we plunge into this final week of study together, I pray that all the discoveries and reminders of Abba's tender, powerful care will converge and fuse with a focus on your inheritance as His cherished child. Before we go any further, please join me in praying the words of Ephesians 1:18: "I pray . . . that the eyes of [our hearts] may be enlightened in order that [we] may know the hope to which he has called [us], the riches of his glorious inheritance in the saints."

# Ponder Scripture

Read the following Scripture passages aloud:

> Praise be to the God and Father of our Lord Jesus Christ!
> In his great mercy he has given us new birth into a living
> hope through the resurrection of Jesus Christ from the
> dead, and into an inheritance that can never perish, spoil
> or fade—kept in heaven for you, who through faith are
> shielded by God's power until the coming of the salvation
> that is ready to be revealed in the last time. (1 Peter 1:3-5)

> You also were included in Christ when you heard the word
> of truth, the gospel of your salvation. Having believed,
> you were marked in him with a seal, the promised Holy
> Spirit, who is a deposit guaranteeing our inheritance until
> the redemption of those who are God's possession—to the
> praise of his glory. (Ephesians 1:13-14)

Please reread the two passages and underline words or phrases that
describe your inheritance. What stands out to you?

Abba's children are guaranteed the ultimate inheritance. It's alive,
vibrant, indestructible, and yours by birth. You're rich! It's free to you,
but it cost your Father the life of His Son. As with any inheritance, there
is a death before the inheritance can be received. But rather than being
accompanied by grief and guilt, this inheritance comes with hope and

joy. Death does not have the final word because of the Resurrection of Jesus. As God's children, we are raised to eternal life with Jesus, to a "living hope . . . [and given] an inheritance that can never perish, spoil or fade" (1 Peter 1:3-4).

Yet the evidence that we still live in the midst of decay and pain is plentiful. It's hard to imagine eternal bliss in the face of regular assaults on our hearts. We still feel the pain of broken relationships and our own failures and see those we love wounded. The apostle Paul felt the daily tension between living in the already and not-yet stage of life too. Read 2 Corinthians 4:7-12 and 16-18. In what ways do you identify with Paul's words?

Take a moment to imagine a perfect day. Where would you be? Who would you be with and what would you eat? How would you spend your time? What colors, sounds, and textures surround you? What would characterize your relationships?

As great as your imagination is, there's more: Your heavenly Father knows every fiber of your being, every hope, every tear and is thoughtfully preparing a place for you that surpasses anything you've ever imagined. Your future is more than bright.

Although we turn waiting and hopeful eyes toward eternity, Abba also holds out strength and grace for today. Life—kingdom life—began in you the moment you became Abba's girl, and that life is meant to be lived in the present as well as in the time to come. Much of what we discover about our inheritance will have fulfillment for you now and hold promise for the future.

## Your New Home

When you see or remember the physical house that you grew up in, what associations, pleasant or distasteful, come to mind? What other places (a lake, park bench, stoop, tree house, and so forth) evoke positive associations?

Holly tells of a friend's house she never wants to leave. Time flies when she's there. It's warm, welcoming, safe, and refreshing, like an oasis in the desert. A shadow of longing is cast on her face as she watches the dad share life with his kids. She sees them laugh and cry together and wants to clone their home and run to its shelter whenever life's demands are overwhelming.

Describe a home you wish you could flee to.

Part of your heritage as a daughter of the King is a safe dwelling place:

You were intended to live in your Father's house. Any place less than His is insufficient. Any place far from His is dangerous. Only the home built for your heart can protect your heart. And your Father wants you to dwell in him.[3]

Look up John 14:2,23; Psalm 90:1; 2 Corinthians 5:1; and Acts 17:28. What aspects about your new home, both present and future, do you find most appealing? What would it feel like to be empowered to invite others home to your Father's house?

Your dwelling place is eternal, but there's also fluid and flexible space available in the now. We can learn to abide more each day in the enfolding presence of God. David, in Psalm 27:4-6, poured out his longing to live out his days in the house of God, gazing upon His beauty. Try making David's words your own and then sit comfortably and quiet your heart, remembering that Abba is right there with you. Imagine for a moment Abba cupping your face in His hands and lifting your head so that your eyes are on Him. Take some time to breathe in the wonder of His presence and just be with Him.

How are you affected by Abba's presence?

Read over the following quote from *The Practice of the Presence of God*:

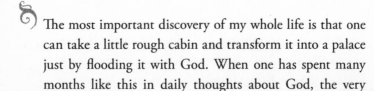

The most important discovery of my whole life is that one can take a little rough cabin and transform it into a palace just by flooding it with God. When one has spent many months like this in daily thoughts about God, the very entering of the house, the very sight of it as one approaches, starts associations which set the heart tingling and the mind flowing.[4]

Consider how God has crafted you. Do you remember best through visuals, sounds, active participation, or some combination? What will help your thoughts return to God's presence throughout the day? Ask Abba to teach you how to live more and more moments in His amazing presence and journal any insights.

## Healed and Whole

The passage we read earlier in 1 Peter 1:3-5 is phrased in *The Message* like this:

> What a God we have! And how fortunate we are to have him, this Father of our Master Jesus! Because Jesus was raised from the dead, we've been given a brand-new life and have everything to live for, including a future in heaven—and the future starts now! God is keeping careful watch over us and the future. The Day is coming when you'll have it all—life healed and whole.

Do you ever feel like Humpty Dumpty, who can never be put together again? We often look around and see our fragments of hope littered with scratches and gaping wounds. All the anguish multiplies until everything feels like a big deal.

Joseph, whose story is told in Genesis 30–50, was hit with one knockout punch after another. Just when it seemed he was going to be okay, he was hit with another left hook. He was a little obnoxious as a youth and made the mistake of reminding his brothers of his favor with their father. His brothers plotted to kill him, stripped him of his prized robe, and threw him into a cistern. They sold him into slavery and let his father, Jacob, believe that he was dead.

Joseph was "betrayed and deserted by his family, exposed to sexual temptation, and punished for doing the right thing; he endured a long imprisonment and was forgotten by those he helped."[5] Even so, Joseph became a man of integrity and wisdom who eventually rose to a position of power in Egypt. Years later his brothers were sent to Egypt during a famine, and "although Joseph recognized his brothers, they did not recognize him" (Genesis 42:8). Ultimately, Joseph helped his father and brothers, arranging for them to live in the best area of Egypt. After Jacob's death and burial, we come upon the scene described in Genesis 50:15-21.

Read this passage, picturing each dramatic moment. List possible emotions and nonverbal cues of Joseph and his brothers:

|  | Emotions | Nonverbals |
|---|---|---|
| Joseph |  |  |
| Joseph's brothers |  |  |

Reread the passage again and pretend you are Joseph. What gives him the power in the midst of his tears to say that God turned all the pain into good? Who has betrayed, bruised, or torn you into pieces? Will you bring each piece to your Father?

Your inheritance as His precious daughter includes restoration. He has the power and tenderness necessary to gather up all the brokenness and set you free to flourish. There is no pain He cannot heal or turn to good.

Read Isaiah 61:1-4 and note which description of living hope and restoration you most need right now. Lay that need before God and lean into the truth of His Word. Ask Him to allow your future to bring hope to your today.

## The Riches of Your Inheritance

Matthew 6:20 says, "Store up for yourselves treasures in heaven, where moth and rust do not destroy, and where thieves do not break in and steal."

Make or purchase a treasure box. It can be as simple as a shoe box or as elaborate as you wish. Place in the box a document listing what has been given to you as a daughter of the King and something to symbolize each item on your list. Be as creative as you like. For example:

- A clean heart: a Valentine or heart necklace
- Identity as a princess: a small tiara
- Home in heaven: a picture of your dream home from a magazine
- Eternal life: a piece of silk greenery
- Salvation: a LifeSaver candy
- Wholeness: _____
- Restoration: _____
- Glory: _____
- Satisfaction: _____
- Security: _____
- Other: _____

Place your treasure box in a place where you will see it and be reminded of your wealth as a child of God.

# Reflect

Ephesians 1:14 says that the Holy Spirit "is a deposit guaranteeing our inheritance." Every discovery, every intimate blessing we have already received and continue to receive is a treasure, but a deeper joy is waiting.

Take in 1 John 3:1-3 and 1 Corinthians 13:12. Purposely savor each word. As fully known children, healed, whole, pure, and drenched in lavish love, we will look into Abba's face. We will see this Father who created, chose, cherished, protected, and comforted us and so much more. Picture the look in Abba's eyes, the beauty of His countenance. Draw a picture of this face-to-face meeting and pour colors onto a page to represent feelings. List words that come to mind, choose flowers for the occasion, or cook a celebratory dinner; do whatever you can to commemorate this amazing moment to come.

If possible, take some time to listen to or download Mercy Me's song "I Can Only Imagine" and use it to celebrate the wonder of your glorious eternal inheritance.

# Respond

I'm not sure there will ever be enough creativity on the planet or sufficient words to respond to the love of the Father. I only hope we never stop trying to "[give] thanks to the Father, who has qualified [us] to share in the inheritance of the saints in the kingdom of light" (Colossians 1:12).

Will you entertain the thought of responding to your Father with a dance of thanksgiving? A recent commercial featured a little girl standing on her daddy's feet as they danced. I'm not sure what was being advertised; I was captivated by the possibility of dancing with my Abba Father. Wouldn't that be an amazing experience?

As a symbol of receiving your inheritance with gratitude, would you accept an invitation to stand on your Father's feet and allow Him to lead you in an eternal dance? Feel Him holding you and leading you through dances in the dark and dances in the light, through the dips and twirls and sways. Embrace today's dance and dream of the future. Picture the day when you can gaze up through your lashes, look Him fully in the face, and dance into eternity enveloped in His love. Play or sing your favorite worship song. This is your own special Father/ daughter moment. Consider literally dancing as you pour out your heart to Him.

Abba powerfully and tenderly leads you today and will be there for all your tomorrows. His arms are wide open inviting you to a forever dance. I pray that each day you will know more of the "hope to which he has called you" (Ephesians 1:18) and, as the song says, "when you have the chance to sit it out or dance, I hope you dance."[6]

# Review

1. Take out your "dream dad" description from week 1 and read it. What has been fulfilled by your heavenly Father?
2. Has your heart begun to absorb the reality of your Abba Father's love? If so, in what ways?
3. In weeks 1 through 5, what scriptures meant the most to you? Why?
4. In weeks 6 through 10, what scriptures meant the most to you? Why?
5. What might your unique Father/daughter dance look like in the coming days?

# Notes

Week 1: Abba Father

1. "Father Me: You Have Loved Me," by Paul Oakley. Copyright 2005, ThankYou Music (adm by Music Services). All rights reserved. Used by permission.
2. Brennan Manning, *Abba's Child: The Cry of the Heart for Intimate Belonging* (Colorado Springs, CO: NavPress, 1994), 62–63.
3. James Strong, LL.D., S.T.D., *The New Strong's Expanded Dictionary of Bible Words* (Nashville: Thomas Nelson, 2001), 905.

Week 2: Chosen to Belong

1. "Out Here on My Own," by Lesley Gore and Michael Gore. Copyright 1980, from the MGM Motion Picture *Fame*.
2. William Barclay, *The New Daily Study Bible Letter to the Romans* (Louisville, KY: Westminster John Knox, 1975), 125.
3. James Strong, LL.D., S.T.D., *The New Strong's Expanded Dictionary of Bible Words* (Nashville: Thomas Nelson, 2001), 1117.
4. "I Will Change Your Name," by D.J. Butler. Copyright 1987, Mercy Publishing (adm by Music Services). All Rights Reserved. Used by permission.

Week 3: The Father's Love

1. "The Love of God," by Frederick M. Lehman, 1917.
2. The Princeton Language Institute, *21st Century Dictionary of Quotations* (New York: Dell, 1993), 270.

3. Oswald Chambers, quoted in Beth Moore, *Praying God's Word: Breaking Free from Spiritual Strongholds* (Nashville: Broadman, Holman, 2003), 96.

4. www.holocaustcenterbuff.com/anna.html.

5. Catherine of Genoa, quoted in Richard Foster and James Bryan Smith, *Devotional Classics: Selected Readings for Individuals and Groups* (New York: HarperCollins, 1993), 181.

## Week 4: In His Arms

1. A. T. Robertson, "Commentary on 2 Corinthians 1:3, *Word Pictures of the New Testament*, http://www.searchgodsword.org/com/rwp/view.cg?book=2cochapter=001verse=003.

2. Corrie Ten Boom with Jamie Buckingham, *Tramp for the Lord* (New York: Jove Books, 1974), 116–117.

3. Adele Ahlberg Calhoun, *Spiritual Disciplines Handbook: Practices That Transform Us* (Downers Grove, IL: InterVarsity, 2005), 205.

## Week 5: Under His Wings

1. John Baillie, *A Diary of Private Prayer* (New York: Simon & Schuster, 1977), 121.

2. "Tupperware Parties of 2007," *Orlando News*, Local 6.com/news, November 12, 2007.

3. Dr. Henry Cloud and Dr. John Townsend, *Boundaries: When to Say Yes, When to Say No to Take Control of Your Life* (Grand Rapids, MI: Zondervan, 1992), 31.

4. Cloud and Townsend, 31.

5. Hannah Whitall Smith, *The Christian's Secret of a Happy Life* (Tarrytown, NY: Revell/Spire, 1952), 42–43.

6. Thomas à Kempis, quoted in Rueben P. Job and Norman Shawchuck, comps., *A Guide to Prayer* (Nashville: The Upper Room, 1983), 98–99.

## Week 6: Through Abba's Eyes

1. *Shrek*, directed by Andrew Adamson and Vicky Jenson (Glendale,

CA: DreamWorks Pictures, 2001).

2. Dallas Willard and Jan Johnson, *Renovation of the Heart in Daily Practice: Experiments in Spiritual Transformation* (Colorado Springs, CO: NavPress, 2006), 119.

3. Ric Ergenbright, *The Art of God* (Wheaton, IL: Tyndale, 1999), 5.

4. Jerusha Clark, *Every Thought Captive: Battling the Toxic Beliefs That Separate Us from the Life We Crave* (Colorado Springs, CO: NavPress, 2006), 162.

5. Federico Fellini, quoted in Danielle DuRant, "The Eyes of God," http://www.rzim.org/USA/USFV/tabid/436/ArticleID/6618/CBModuleID/881/Default.aspx.

6. Sam Levenson, "Time Tested Beauty Tips," http://www.robinsweb.com/inspiration/beauty_tips.html.

Week 7: A Generous Father

1. Patricia Zimmerman, *My Father Gave Me a Serpent* (Old Tappan, NJ: Chosen Books, 1986).

2. Michael J. Wilkins, *The NIV Application Commentary: Matthew* (Grand Rapids, MI: Zondervan, 2004), 313.

3. David G. Benner, *Desiring God's Will: Aligning Our Hearts with the Heart of God* (Downers Grove, IL: InterVarsity, 2005), 39.

4. Mark Buchanan, *The Holy Wild: Trusting in the Character of God* (Sisters, OR: Multnomah, 2003), 170.

5. David Hazard, comp., *A Day in Your Presence: A 40-Day Journey in the Company of Francis of Assisi* (Minneapolis: Bethany, 1992), 21.

Week 8: A Daughter's Inheritance

1. Rosamund Stone Zander and Benjamin Zander, *The Art of Possibility: Transforming Professional and Personal Life* (New York: Penguin Books, 2000), 26–27.

2. C. S. Lewis, *The Weight of Glory* (New York: HarperCollins, 1976), 26.

3. Max Lucado, *The Great House of God* (Dallas: Word, 1997), 3.
4. Brother Lawrence and Frank Laubach, *The Practice of the Presence of God*, Library of Spiritual Classics, vol. 1 (Jacksonville, FL: SeedSowers Publishing, 1973), 18.
5. *Life Application Study Bible NIV* (Wheaton, IL: Tyndale/ Zondervan, 1991), 77.
6. "I Hope You Dance," by Lee Ann Womack. Copyright 2000, Nashville: MCA.

# About the Author

Rita Platt is a speaker, writer, and workshop leader who focuses on delighting in and experiencing deeper relationship with God. She is passionate about knowing the Lord with her head and her heart and inspiring others to walk in intimate relationship with Him. She is currently pursuing an MA in professional counseling with an emphasis on soul care. She is a certified Prepare/Enrich premarital and marital counselor. Rita holds a BA in communication, has a certificate in women and evangelism from the Billy Graham Center, and is a trained infant-adoption liaison. She also participated in an intensive week of training at the Leighton Ford Evangelism Leadership Conference.

Rita served for years as counseling coordinator at the Colorado Springs Pregnancy Center. She wrote materials for use in training and in the counseling room, including a brochure titled *Reflections for Your Journey*, used to introduce women to the Lord. The *Reflections* brochure was translated into Russian for use in some pregnancy centers in Russia. Rita has also served in church ministry as a child and family ministry director initiating and creating new programs. She is a trained Parenting with Love and Logic facilitator and has authored articles titled "Silent Release" and "Advice for Parents of Prodigals." In addition, Rita served as worship leader for a single moms' ministry.

Rita, her husband, Thom, and Schipperke puppy, Lucy, recently relocated from Colorado Springs, Colorado, to Columbia, Maryland. Rita loves and is involved in music, performance art, and visual arts. Her hobbies include photographing waterfalls, knitting, and reading.

# Other Bible studies from Rita Platt and more!

### An Undivided Heart
Rita Platt
978-1-60006-388-6
Jesus wants to know you intimately. Enter an eternal romance with Jesus that moves beyond mere sentimentality. This eight-week study includes review and discussion questions.

### Step into the Waters
Rita Platt
978-160006-389-3
Let your heart experience the abundant flow of living water and immerse yourself in life-giving intimacy with the Spirit. In *Step into the Waters*, women can connect deeply with the Holy Spirit through Scripture, personal stories, discussion questions, and spiritual disciplines. This eight-week study includes review and discussion questions.

### The Amazing Collection
Big Dream Ministries, Inc.
THE AMAZING COLLECTION is a DVD Bible study taught book by book. The forty-five-minute DVDs with workbooks bring the main characters and the theme of each book of the Bible alive with dynamic teaching, original music videos, and personal testimonies.